Why the Private School?

In 1945 The Tuition Plan established the Educational Research Fund to do independent research in the field of education. This book is the third sponsored by the Fund. The first two were:

ADMISSION TO AMERICAN COLLEGES
by Benjamin Fine

BEHIND THE ACADEMIC CURTAIN
by Archibald MacIntosh

WHY the PRIVATE SCHOOL?

ALLAN V. HEELY

HEAD MASTER, THE LAWRENCEVILLE SCHOOL

HARPER & BROTHERS · PUBLISHERS · NEW YORK

To Pattie

CONTENTS

PREFACE

This book is one man's observations about the private school. It is subjective and personal. It expresses his convictions, opinions, and biases and nothing else.

The original concept of the book was more ambitious. It was recommended at first that I address myself to a consideration of the role of secondary education, both public and private, in the United States—a task, in point of time and competence, beyond my grasp.

After the sights had been set to focus on the private, or independent, school alone, I was advised to approach its function in America as a social historian would do, expounding its qualities objectively and dispassionately, gathering all manner of statistical material to support my findings. From this I was inhibited by temperament and training.

So the book has become what one man thinks. But I have not worked alone on it. I was counseled at the outset by the members of the Advisory Committee of the Educational Research Fund of The Tuition Plan, which invited me to write it. I owe much to many others. Some of them I have mentioned in the text of the book. Mr. M. Roy Ridley, my Oxford tutor and recent colleague at Lawrenceville, will recognize what I have used of his without acknowledgement. From the rest, whose oral and written comments on my undertaking were offered with generosity and insight, I have borrowed ideas shamelessly and gratefully. I ally myself with all of them in purpose and devotion, and I regard my association with them as one of the great rewards of our profession. My special thanks go to Miss Terry Ferrer for suggesting the title. For most of the material in Chapter X I am indebted to Dr. Benjamin H. Balser, Psychiatric Consultant to the Lawrenceville School.

The book falls short of what I think is adequate. I hope, however, that it may prove suggestive and so beget its betters.

ALLAN V. HEELY

Lawrenceville, New Jersey
November, 1950

PART ONE

The Place of the Private School

CHAPTER I

"All Men Are Created Equal"

Today in America the private school is asking itself questions. If it asks the right ones and gets the right answers, the effect ought to be therapeutic. For the independent school enjoys the peculiar advantage that it can be as good as it wants to be, if it can find out what that is. The process of self-examination will also be painful. For custom rides hard upon the consciences of men; and what you have always done is likely to seem therefore good and quite possibly so good that it could not be better.

The subject of the discussion is the function of the private school in American education. By reason of the nature of my business, I have read a lot about it and listened to a lot more; not to speak of the fuel I myself have added to the flame. I confess that much of it now seems to me irrelevant and inconclusive, and some of it prejudiced, defensive, and absurd; though the question itself I believe to be an important one, and certainly I have more than a passing interest in it.

The trouble with the controversy is that it has a tendency to start at the wrong place. It tries to define a function without first clarifying the end it is to serve. Now, you cannot establish the value of a part if you lift it out of its context, for outside the context it can have no value. The context of the private school is the whole program of American education, of which it is a part. Its function is subservient to a national objective; its value contingent upon how well it performs it. The question to start with, therefore, is the function of education as a whole in a democracy. And you cannot begin to answer that until some agreement has been reached on what the democracy means and what it intends to do for the people who compose it.

In the sort of society that Hitler and Stalin have considered desirable, democracy means the extinction of individual freedom of action, thought, and speech in the interests of the state as those interests have been determined and announced by its leaders; what the democracy intends to do for the people who compose it is to juggernaut them. The function of education in such a democracy is therefore attractively clear and simple. It consists in the dispensing of ideas and the imposition of facts which appeal to the authorities as convenient and, to the national ego, exhilarating. There is no clash of opinion over the policies and the practices of education, for there is only one opinion. People who disagree and say so have a tendency to get lost, often permanently.

Despite a distressing ignorance and confusion on the subject, the meaning of the American democracy and what it intends to do for the people who compose it are equally clear, though by no means so simple and considerably more fatiguing. They are contained in the Declaration of Independence and the Constitution.

The first impressive feature of the Declaration is that it was unanimous: a consummation suggesting long and careful thought by a group of superior persons: for it is a document far beyond the reach of mediocrity. The kind of democracy these men envisioned affirmed as "self-evident" the "truths" that "all men are created equal" and enjoy, by a gift of God, "certain unalienable rights," which are not extensively enumerated, but which include the right to "life, liberty, and the pursuit of happiness." Near the end of their statement they appealed to "the Supreme Judge of the world" for the rectitude of their intentions. They said further that they entertained "a firm reliance on the protection of Divine Providence." And toward the support of their declaration they finally pledged their lives, their fortunes, and their sacred honor. In other words, they staked all they had and all they were on a government of individual freedom under God; and since it has never been suggested that they were being disingenuous or facetious, those of us who are interested in American education would seem bound to take them seriously.

These men represented and spoke, in protest and affirmation, for the colonies "in General Congress assembled." In this capacity they dealt with principles and ends. The writers of the Constitution, on the other hand, were concerned with means. They were charged with the formulation of a system of government which would effectuate the demands and the aspirations espoused by the Declaration. The Constitution, therefore, is precise where the Declaration is general. Government under the Constitution, for example, does not, as the Declaration does, rely on "the protection of Divine Providence." Neither does it repudiate it. It merely prohibits any religious test as a qualification for office, or any legally constituted religious establishment, or any restraint upon the free exercise of religion; the securing of freedom being the great desideratum—a proposition with which it may be supposed the writers of the Declaration would have agreed, particularly since six men signed both documents.

That is to say that, despite differences in emphasis and purpose between the two instruments, the rights affirmed were the rights secured. Since its ratification the Constitution, to be sure, has been repeatedly amended in matters of procedure and in the interests of greater clarity. But the most important of the amendments comprises the Bill of Rights, which is devoted entirely to the rights of individuals; and the end of freedom and equality which the Constitution was designed to secure has remained basic and unimpugned, held to be valid and essential by all shades of political, social, and economic opinion. What the American democracy means and what it intends to do for Americans have been once and for all time made clear.

On the basis of that meaning and those intentions it becomes possible to discuss the role of education in America. I suggest that it has two parts.

Its first business is to teach all Americans to understand the ends of the American commitment and the methods by which it may be realized; to give them—all of them—the means of making their lives personally satisfying and vocationally effective; and to dispose them, as citizens, workers, and members of families, to contribute their capacities to the elevation of the common life.

The task of teaching all Americans to understand their democracy and to realize their part in it requires first that everybody must be taught how to read and, as far as his native capacity permits, to understand what he reads. Deceptively simple as this sounds, it is in execution a task of peculiar difficulty. The common notion that "of course everyone who has been to school can read" stems from uninspected assumption rather than from grasp of fact. For though it would not be likely to occur to anybody that he himself could not read, when obviously he did it all the time, the fact is that a deplorably large number of secondary school graduates—and college alumni too, for that matter—can read with understanding only relatively elementary material. Along with reading should go training in writing and speaking; neither of them in a professional or vocational sense, but only to the end that, if a man has an idea or an opinion, he may be able to write it or say it exactly and intelligibly. These needs are paramount for the reason that the citizens of our democracy must be trained to understand each other, so that when they talk or write or read or listen there may be the assurance of a real interchange of ideas, of genuine communication.

In a country where the right to vote is widely distributed, democratic education must also train electors who will know what they are voting for, who can apprehend what editors and candidates for office are saying to them, and who can tell the difference between a leader and a demagogue. If our people are to conduct themselves with maximum effectiveness as citizens, they ought further to know something of the background of the political, social, and economic history of their country; for their ignorance will turn to gullibility if they suppose that the headlines in the morning paper refer to problems that have no past, but only an obscure present and a future that is anybody's guess.

If our schools are to fulfill their further responsibility to give all the people the means of making their lives personally satisfying, they must try to awaken in them a response to literature, music, and the graphic arts, suiting both material and methods of instruction to the needs and the capacities of their students. The purpose of this effort is not to impose upon the people a veneer of "culture." It is to make them aware of some of the sources from which they may derive recreation and enrichment after the burden and the heat of the economic, civic, and family day.

In addition to guiding carefully the vocational selections of their pupils, our schools are bound to provide for them the sort of specific vocational preparation that their intentions and their competence suggest, whether they propose to occupy themselves manually or professionally or otherwise.

And the capstone of the structure—hard to design and harder to effectuate—is the inculcation, in all who have been taught, of a purpose to apply their various talents to the improvement of the communities in which they may live, regarding their privileges as involving them in inescapable responsibilities. For the education of the American people is aimed not merely at individual embellishment. It is aimed at individual enlightenment. And enlightenment is not knowledge or skill or accomplishment; it is spiritual, emotional, and intellectual temper and perception.

The Declaration of Independence is concerned with ideals. Ideals express values. If our schools, therefore, are to teach Americans to be "good citizens," they must find a way to make values permeate the consciences and inspire the actions of their graduates; and they must decide precisely in advance what values they wish to implant and how they propose to go about it. They must manage to convey the recognition that "good" has not only a material meaning—appropriate, for example, in speaking of a "good" chair or a "good" automobile—but a moral meaning also, which is intended to communicate the idea of a "good" man. And they must teach the people how to tell which is which.

These are minimum objectives, probably inadequate, certainly incomplete. Omitted from them, for example, is the place of religion in American education, which I shall undertake to discuss later. Some such training for everybody, however, I conceive to be the only means by which free men can be prepared to exercise their privileges and their obligations; the only means by which the sort of democratic American society envisioned by our founders can be realized.

The second great business of education in the American democracy can be more briefly stated. It is to identify at an early age those of the people whose qualities are exceptional and so to train them as to develop their capacities to the full.

In both these national undertakings it is the individual who is to be made the center of focus. American democratic principle is a blunt repudiation of the concept that there is any such thing as the masses and the classes, which is the particular obsession of the Marxian philosophy. American education is to accomplish the full capitalization of individual resources. Its worth is therefore to be judged by its quality rather than by its quantity, and the index of its quality is its degree of success in effecting the maximum extension of human potentialities.

These two educational objectives—the provision for all the people of a superior preparation for their lives as citizens and the more specialized training of the exceptional minority—are both a national responsibility of which all properly qualified girls and boys should be the beneficiaries. Since the Civil War the public secondary schools have rapidly taken over the task of administering education for all the people, training them as citizens and fitting them for vocations or for further formal education. The fact that there are now more than twenty-five thousand such schools in the country indicates the magnitude of the enterprise. Schools conducted under private auspices also have had a hand in this undertaking, with results more impressive than the relatively insignificant number of students involved would lead one to suppose.

The proper education of the superior minority, which is the second major responsibility of democratic education, has been dealt with far less successfully than the first. "Superior" is a word with emotional connotations. It implies clearly that if someone is superior, somebody else must be inferior; and though that is a plain fact, it is in America a particularly unpalatable one, unless carefully explained and qualified. Its significance, therefore, is obscured by the frustrating, illusive intangibles that color men's perception of what some words plainly mean; or, paradoxically, do not mean at all. This semantic confusion is a vexing problem to our whole program of American education. For by reason of the lack of a clear and continuing agreement about what words mean, by reason of the individual emotional preoccupations that make the same word mean different things to different people, we may defeat our ends, or at least retard our progress toward them, while we are earnestly seeking to advance and secure them.

To many Americans, for example, the declaration that "all men are created equal" has meant the guarantee of equality not only of opportunity, but also of achievement, as though all men would somehow come out equal if they were given an equal chance and really worked hard. This, of course, is equalitarianism run amuck. In physical, mental, and spiritual equipment people take their places between the widest conceivable extremes. Education must recognize these differences, must indeed base itself upon them, if it is to accomplish its democratic function.

Men are equal, or ought to be, before the law and in the sight of God. But it is neither the law nor God which the

Jacksonian progeny have in mind when they contend that
the attempt on the part of education to recognize and accommodate differences in ability would threaten our society
with division into classes and with a consequent inequality of
privilege based on class distinctions. It is rather a fear of the
stigma of inferiority, publicly made manifest, that presses
education in this country to level down to mediocrity, where
everyone is comfortably as "good" as everyone else. It
ought to be clearer to us than it evidently is that, if a man's
freedom is to be any "good" to him or to the country, it
must mean freedom to develop all his capacities to the top
of their bent; not at all at the expense of his fellows, but
rather as an affirmation of their own right to the same freedom. Let it be said at the outset, therefore, that the chief
danger to which American education is today vulnerable is
the danger of contentment with mediocrity; which is therefore also the chief threat to the quality of American society.

The fact is that no democracy can realize its full potentialities unless its plan of education looks toward the cultivation of its superior minority, of an aristocracy of brains
with character. The leadership of the state, not merely in
politics but in all the walks of life, should be vested in the
best individuals the state can produce; not best in the sense
of moral worth (though they are likely to be that too), but
best in the possession of the qualities that are essential to
distinction of performance in any calling—which are clearly
not the monopoly of any class. The sort of democracy intended by the Declaration of Independence and implemented
by the Constitution has in view the freedom of every citizen
to rise, in his chosen field of effort, to the highest level that
his ability permits; and this freedom would be useless indeed
in the absence of means for sifting out the best, developing
their powers to the full, and securing that there be no bar,

social or financial, which might prevent this best minority from being selected and trained. There is nothing "undemocratic" about this sort of special training provided it is made available to everybody on the basis of merit only. On the contrary, a democracy which neglects, in its system of education, to provide for each the true measure of his capacities cannot escape the dominance of the mediocre.

Now, it is important to observe that these leaders are not to be autocrats or dictators. For, in contrast to other kinds of states, the American democracy intends that the people as a whole—"we the people"—shall control their own affairs. The leaders are to lead, not to control by aristocratic edict. This condition requires leaders trained not in brain only, but in the sort of human understanding that will permit them to sense and to sympathize with—and to guide with insight and humility—the impulses and aspirations of their fellow citizens. To secure such leadership every American, whatever the kind and quality of his ability, must receive the sort of education that will enable him to clarify his opportunities and his responsibilities as a citizen, understand the issues that affect him, and cooperate informedly in their advancement.

Let it be repeated: this is not "class" education in any objectionable sense. It is the only means by which education in the American democracy can make fully available the various capacities of all its citizens. It should be the basic tenet of American education that there can be no conflict between democracy and distinction. It is shamefully clear that we have permitted the conflict to permeate our practice, while denying its existence as a matter of principle. We have in fact discriminated against races and creeds and colors, and against social and economic groups. We have been too often satisfied with mediocrity, if not indeed eager to accommodate it; and if we do not change our ways, there will be no health in us.

It is a matter, in brief, of the parable of the talents, whose relevance to American education is generally ignored. They were distributed "to every man according to his several ability," with no suggestion that a man with more talents than another was a "better" man. It was what he did with what he had that alone counted. It is the task of democratic education to discover each person's ability, and to nourish and cultivate it as a thing of special worth. But the demagogic insistence that one talent is as "good" as five and an educational program shaped to fit such patent obscurantism is perverse and stultifying. The most damaging mistake democratic education can make is to waste the brains of the ablest or, conversely, to place mediocrity in positions of leadership for which it is clearly unfit. The fact that we have too often done precisely that is at the heart of our present educational dilemma.

The proper education of the superior individual imposes special conditions. It demands, first of all, the devising of reliable instruments of measurement which can be counted on to mark out who the superior individuals are. The present standard tests of scholastic aptitude and achievement are by themselves inadequate for this purpose. Furthermore, academic aptitude should not be the single criterion for such selection. Qualities of personality and character deserve equal consideration; and there is a large number of potentially superior citizens whose intelligence quotients would sadden a university director of admissions.

In the second place, the superior boy or girl should be segregated for instructional purposes. This notion is repugnant to a good many thoughtful people whose dedication to the cause of education is unquestionable. Their belief is that in American schools any such differentiation is undemocratic. It suggests, they contend, an invidious distinction between the intellectual "haves" and "have nots" and gives rise to painful feelings of social inferiority. In order to hold this view with confidence and firmness, it is necessary to ignore its inconsistency. It is inconsistent because everybody knows that both the standards of classroom instruction and the methods used to achieve them must be and always are different for various levels of mental capacity: that no one would think of teaching English or arithmetic or history or science (and some of all these subjects must be taught to all children if they are merely to understand their role as citizens) to all students in the same way or with the same materials or under the same scheme of evaluation. In short, all effective teaching, whatever its field, must be and always has been conformed to the recognition of the native capacity of those who are to be taught—that is to say, to the principle of differentiation. And nobody objects to it in general.

The extracurricular activities of a school, indeed, are not only expected to practice it, but are strongly criticized if they do not. No parent feels that his *amour propre* has been wounded if his child fails to make the football team or the glee club or the board of editors of the school newspaper. In such enterprises there is rigorous and unqualified discrimination in favor of native ability. The more rigorous and unqualified the discrimination, the higher the quality of performance. And the higher the quality of performance, the greater the prestige of the activity.

Furthermore, in the course of more than a quarter century of work in college preparatory schools, I have never met parents who expressed a preference for the attendance of their children at easy or middle-rate colleges or professional schools. They always want the best. And the only reason why the ones they want *are* the best is that their standards of admission are based on superior capacities and on them alone. It is hard to understand, therefore, why such parents should often be content with less at the school level, where the foundation for all further study must be laid.

The fact is, of course, that the separation of students for curricular purposes on the basis of ability is not opposed, on the whole, by the parents of superior children. They are glad to have them really challenged. The opposition comes from the parents of children on the lower levels of mental capacity, who are socially embarrassed by the fact that the children of their friends are sometimes placed higher in the academic scale. Even these protestants do recognize, of course, that people differ in ability, as they do in height and strength and complexion; and as a general rule they themselves feel superior to certain of their fellow citizens and freely say so. But they are unprepared, in point of emotional maturity and intellectual detachment, to accept the application of the plain facts to their own sons and daughters; and so they deny the facts and press for what they call equality. In so doing they may save face in their social communities, even though the truth will out somewhere along the line. But they also lend their support to the dominance of the average in American education; and this, because it limits the ablest in their freedom to excel, constitutes a denial of the very democratic principle by which it is defended.

In short, I am pleading merely for the same practice in the classroom as everywhere else. The reluctance of the American public, on grounds of "democratic equality," to accept this practice must result in the fact that everybody suffers. Every teacher knows this who has taught a group of students whose range of ability was wide. He must either spend his time enlightening the mediocre, in which case the superior pupils are bored and properly inattentive; or, if he concentrates on stretching the capacities of the ablest, he must expect bewilderment, frustration, and finally resentment on the part of the rest. Or, if he tries to do both, he and the whole group with him fall between two stools. It is like asking a football coach to teach varsity stars and third-string substitutes all at once. In both cases nobody gets the kind of instruction he needs or can profit by; nobody's latent ability is fully developed.

Finally, the education of exceptional capacity must go forward under standards of such rigor as to stretch the mind to capacity performance.

Now, I am not advocating the institution of intellectual hothouses at the secondary school level. As I have already said, other qualities than innate mental superiority should govern the selection of the outstanding group: such as leadership, personality, strength of will and purpose, the ability to perceive social objectives, and the eager disposition to contribute to their advancement. I am saying that, if it is to fulfill its function, American education must discover the capacities, the needs, the purposes, the ambitions of each child and then set up facilities good enough to meet them. The American tradition of equality of educational opportunity must always be observed. But you cannot observe it by ignoring the specifications I am urging; indeed, "opportunity" can have no useful meaning to a citizen unless it secures for him the full extension of his special powers.

The way to observe it is to see to it that the chance to move from one social or economic situation to another in our society is kept free and fluid for everyone on the basis of individual capacity, regardless of race, creed, color, religion, wealth, social position, or any other irrelevant consideration. That is the unique and noble basis of the American credo, and it is disturbing to notice that in the people's schools pressure is being exerted to dilute it in the interests of a specious equalitarianism. In American education "best" should mean simply "best fitted"; and in that meaning it should apply equally to all vocations.

In this matter of the education of the superior student, I cannot join with those of my professional colleagues who believe that, although the present situation in American schools is unsatisfactory, it is more important to avoid differentiation than it is to do anything radical by way of improvement.

I do not share their fear that the segregation of the best will inevitably result in the cultivation of prigs or academic snobs. My own experience in private schools does not support their contention. On the contrary, I find that men and women of high qualities are likely to be—and for the very reason that they are so distinguished—exceptional in their charity, their humility and simplicity, their sensitivity to others, their wish to be of service, their social sympathies. The primary objective of education is the realization of individual capacities. The problem is not to do the best you can without differentiation. The problem is to do the best you can. I do not pretend that there is any single sacrosanct curriculum for the proper nourishment of the unusually able person, but I should insist that what you teach him and how well make an important difference in the quality of the product. In consequence, I cannot share the cheer of those of my brethren who observe that the brilliant boy and girl may be expected to do exceptional work, however badly they have been taught before. "I eat the air, promise-crammed" is a slogan hardly likely to reassure the able student, however often he repeats it to himself. "You cannot feed capons so." No, nor people of superior ability, either.

CHAPTER II

"The Problem Is To Do the Best You Can"

The question of how and where the requirements of education for distinction can best be met is grave and portentous. On every side one hears and reads dissatisfaction with the present situation, but there is little evidence of planning, of the formulation of broad policy. This is a matter that transcends the special claims or interests of private or public schools or teachers. It calls for conference rather than for controversy. For there is at stake nothing less than the full and effective utilization of the country's total educational resources. In charge of them are thousands of thoughtful teachers and administrators who are already at one in their devotion to the cause of perfecting American education; and this unity of commitment might be made the basis of a closer agreement on the means by which it may be given effect.

At present even the unity of commitment is more often concealed than evident. For in the relationships between the public and the private schools there is a breech which needs to be healed. The public schools are bearing the brunt of the educational battle, often under conditions difficult to bear and unheard-of in the private schools. It is grinding, grueling work, and it is a public service of the first rank. But there is undeniably a tendency on the part of many private school teachers to look down their noses a little at the public school, to feel that it is a bit vulgar and strident and unwashed; and to believe that those who teach in it are somehow not quite up to snuff. And on the part of public school teachers there is often the belief that the private school plumes itself on what it takes to be its social superiority; that it is smug and complacent and ivory-towered; that it does not speak the language or meet the problems of the people; that it "has it soft." The ease with which this ignorance and prejudice break down before a little fellowship and understanding points the direction that both groups ought to follow.

The present situation has prompted President Conant to observe that the private secondary school is "only a specialized competitor with the public high school." And to the extent that others agree with him, his comment calls attention to the degree to which the two kinds of schools are working at cross-purposes with each other, to our national planlessness in education; for it is by no means true in reality. To suppose that the problems of the public school, its challenges, its duties, and its opportunities, let alone its privileges, overlap those of the private school is to disregard facts.

Much harm is also done to the cause of unity by the failure of patrons of the private schools to concern themselves with the quality of their local public schools. I have often heard parents say that they were compelled to send their children to school away from home because the local public schools were inferior. But I do not have the impression that they were disturbed about them, as they should have been, let alone that they were engaged in working for their improvement. I have even known parents to oppose a raise in the tax rate, intended to improve the quality of local public schools, who at the same time were sending their children to expensive private schools. All this makes for bitterness and antagonism, to everybody's hurt.

Perhaps the most serious point of cleavage between the two types of schools is found in their different attitudes toward professional education. It is customary among private school teachers to hold a low opinion of courses in education in particular and of teachers' colleges in general. "You can't teach a teacher how to teach," they say; "teachers are born and not made." Some teachers' colleges are, to be sure, grossly inferior, like some private and public schools. Some public school systems pay more attention to professional courses than to teaching ability. And some private schools teach very well indeed whose faculties grade low in point of professional preparation. But it is easy for the private schools to find the kind of teachers they want, though there are never enough of them to go round, and though some of the most promising candidates turn out to be failures. And even conceding that the best private school teachers do not need to take courses in how to teach, many of them would profit immensely by a knowledge of the new materials and methods in their fields which the professional schools and journals provide.

But the main point is that, during the mushroom growth of public secondary education throughout the United States, teachers had to be provided rapidly and in large numbers. You couldn't wait for "born teachers" to turn up. There weren't enough of them. You had to recruit willing teacher-candidates and do the best you could for and with them. Reliable statistics point to a further rapid expansion of the public school population in the near future, which means that the recruitment of teachers must still go forward apace. The training of teachers for our common schools is a task of staggering proportions. I am not aware that the private school has felt a proper concern about it or has attempted to shoulder a share of the responsibility. The problem has been met by normal schools and, more recently, by teachers' colleges. The cause of unity in American education could be served well if private school teachers and administrators should interest themselves in and contribute to the improvement of the agencies charged with the preparation of teachers for the public schools, which is the most important educational undertaking in the country. And the private schools themselves should use every means at their disposal to strengthen and assist the public schools in the communities they also serve.

As a first step toward the reality of unity, the National Association of Independent Schools suggests that heads of such schools join their state association of principals, attend its meetings, and, as opportunity offers, take part in its programs and committee work. The model for such common effort might well be the Headmasters Association, which for more than fifty years has brought together, in annual fellowship, heads of both public and private schools. They are friends as well as professional colleagues, and they meet in unity, with no sense of separateness.

I observed at the outset that the context of the private school is the whole program of American education; that its function is subservient to a national objective; and that its value is contingent upon how well it performs it. What, then, is its function?

It is obvious that it can play only a numerically insignificant part in the major project of preparing the people for sound citizenship. The private school cannot do *anything* for *everybody*; which, if it be its limitation, is also its opportunity. It can do nothing useful for *anybody*, of course, if it wraps itself in aloof and solitary pride, regarding itself as apart from, rather than a part of, a great national movement. If, on the other hand, it feels itself to be the servant of a public responsibility administered by private funds, it has important potential assets in the balance sheet of the education of the American people. For as an instrument for the education of the carefully selected superior student, the private school is already committed to ends and has at its disposal means which may be adapted to that purpose above all others.

Obviously it enjoys and may utilize certain advantages which stem from the very fact that it is independent: that it is free from some of the circumscriptions within which the tax-supported schools must operate.

It has the advantage of selectivity. It can decide whom to admit and whom not to admit; it can limit its choice to those best equipped to meet its purposes; and it is free to set high standards, the more so because the span of ability represented by its student body is relatively narrow.

It is also free to decide who shall teach and who shall not teach, on the basis of its own judgment alone. The selection and appointment of its teachers are completely within its discretion, beyond the influence of elected or appointed boards of education or of parental pressure. It is free to rid itself of teachers who prove ineffective; free, that is to say, from the limitations of laws regarding tenure; though it ought to make its successful teachers feel secure, and it regards a rapid turnover in its teaching force as a reproach and an affliction. Thus it can match the capacity of its students with a correspondingly high quality of instruction. It is free to make it so and free to keep it so.

It is beyond the reach of textbook purges instigated by fanatical minorities. It can teach what it wants to teach, and its freedom of speech and opinion is immune to public regulation.

These are the chief requirements for excellence in any learning situation.

Fortunately, also, it can provide instruction to small groups of students. There is some debate among schoolteachers as to the relative desirability, in the interests of the most effective teaching, of classroom sections of various sizes. Certainly there is no charmed number which can be proved to assure the best results; too many intangible factors are involved. But the general merit of relatively small sections is perhaps most convincingly attested by public school teachers whose classes, they often say, are too large to permit them to give their best instruction. And for the real meeting of superior minds, for the fruitful interchange of views, for the careful weighing of evidence leading toward sound conclusions, the smaller the group, the better the outcome. As a corollary to its small sections and as a further refinement of its educational process, the private school finds it possible to arrange its classroom sections on the basis of degrees of ability, which is desirable as a means of securing for each student the utmost searching and challenging of his powers.

In my experience with parents, boys, and teachers, all but those who oppose the separate instruction of the ablest on the ground that it is inherently undemocratic would regard the facilities I have described as approaching the ideal.

These advantages do not automatically become realities, of course, merely because such schools are private. If they did, every private school would be a good school, a phenomenon which no sensible person expects ever to contemplate. But they are present as potentialities *in a situation which can be controlled by its administrators*; and they cannot be had otherwise.

In any enterprise, success in reaching its objectives is contingent upon this ability to control the conditions necessary to their achievement. It is impossible to bake a cake or build a house or run a business—or carry out a plan of education—unless the right materials and methods can be counted on and their operation carefully supervised. The private school can control its internal situation. (It cannot, of course, control the economic climate in which it lives.) In the public schools the pressure of numbers has resulted inescapably in the relaxation of their dominance of the conditions under which they would wish to operate. The materials and methods are at hand. The ability to control them is in abeyance.

There are private schools—and far too many of them—which prostitute their opportunities in the priesthood of a god of expediency whose idols are full enrollment, a balanced budget, and a gratifying social reputation. By the same token, there are public schools whose facilities for the education of the especially able are unsurpassed. But these are public schools which have it so, being denied the freedom to make it so. These are schools which, as the wheel of fortune spins, find themselves called upon to serve the needs of a community of exceptional caliber; find that those whom they *must* take are those also whom they would like to take.

There is, nevertheless, wide support of the conviction that the education of the particularly gifted is the proper province of the public school, that it should be provided at public expense, and that it should be offered to everybody without further cost, as a necessary service to the American democracy. The conviction is sound. It ought to be so. Our educational establishment is committed, as a matter of dogma, to the proposition that individual capacities must be nurtured and ripened, as the only means of providing real equality of opportunity. And by the nature of things, our public schools will continue to receive the overwhelming majority of our most talented boys and girls, for private education, in the foreseeable future, will always be expensive.

But on the face of it, if the conditions described above as requisite to the preparation of our superior minority are held to be valid, they cannot by and large be met at present by our public schools. Men who are immersed in promoting the improvement of American public education—some of them inclined to be contemptuous of the use and value of the private school—confess that the public school largely ignores the needs of the exceptional student. It is possible, they say, that this condition is temporary; that as financial support for public schools is adequately increased, they will be able to meet the required conditions and fulfill the function. But some of the wisest of them declare that they do not at present observe, taking the country as a whole, reassuring evidence that a concerted movement is afoot toward that end; that there is no emergent support for a hope that public schools are approaching the achievement of an educational situation which they can fully control.

In an address delivered before a meeting of the Private School Teachers Association of Philadelphia in 1945, Dr. F. H. Bair, of the New York State Bureau of Secondary Education, had this to say about the problem:

In my judgment, the best of the private schools are destined to play an even greater part in the future of this country than they have in its past. These ways arise because the processes of democracy present a perennial paradox: in raising the average, we tend to depress the excellent. But even more significant, in standardizing to improve the educational level of all the people, we tend more and more to stereotype our public schools and more and more to centralize their controls.

I have remarked to some of you before that a great school must be a free school—an unique, living and growing organism.

One increasingly important advantage of the private school is precisely that, except in the most general way, it is not required to conform to or be part of a "system." It is clearly essential to genuinely democratic theory and practice for schools to exist in our society which are free to develop, and do develop, without the stereotyping effects of increasing rigid state and federal controls. Public schools are subject to a lengthening chain of such: teacher tenure, which, so far, makes it next to impossible for a school to rid itself of a merely mediocre instructor; teacher organization for self-centered, as against professional ends; curricular impositions by screwball minorities through legislation; state and federal aid with strings attached; civil service taking over janitorial, clerical and secretarial appointments, and presumably due to spread. All of these things have their good points, against the general background that produced them, but, in the effort to build a great school, taken together they amount to a kind of creeping paralysis. State and federal controls, and public school uniformity and conformity therewith, are, in my judgment, going to increase, and in exact proportion will increase the importance of private schools of sharply marked, long tested character.

The most taxing problem facing our public schools is that of gradually ridding themselves, one community after another, from such regimentation by external imposition, to the end that the exceptional minority may receive their due. As such, it becomes also the most taxing and crucial problem of all those who have a place or an interest in American education. Left to the natural course of events, the problem seems certain to grow worse rather than better. Even today American public schools are getting a financial support wholly inadequate to provide the sort of instructional conditions they would like to have for the education of everybody, let alone of the most gifted. They need large additional sums of money for the improvement merely of their present undertakings. All evidence supports the conviction that the demands to be made upon them in the future will augment their difficul-

ties. The rise in the infant population due to marriages con-
tracted during World War II will result in an increased
school population of formidable magnitude which is already
being realized at the lower grade levels. The future need,
therefore, is not alone to secure funds for the improvement
of the *status quo*; it is to finance a public obligation which,
unless public money becomes available in unprecedented and
almost astronomical volume, may well grow out of hand.

Consideration of the present and a sensible judgment of
the future point toward the conviction that the careful separation of pupils by the measurement of their capacities and the
provision of small instructional units are and will be, in the
public schools, prohibitively expensive. The taxpayers, therefore, could hardly pay for them if they would. And it is
a rueful but inescapable conclusion that, in consequence of
our American predisposition toward lip service to public
education and indifference to its quality, they would not if
they could. For, though the movement for the support of
public education by federal subsidy is fortunately gaining
both momentum and advocacy, it is disheartening to observe
that the talk is all about quantity and not at all of quality.
And what does it profit a community if it spend twice as much
per year per pupil for something which is not demonstrably
better, but only more expensive?

In consequence of its loss of control over its own working
conditions, our program of public schooling involves at
present an appalling waste of potentialities, and the means
suggested to check it are themselves dubious.

In an article in *The New York Times* for October 9, 1949,
Dr. Benjamin Fine, Education Editor, pointed out that of
the 1,700,000 children who had entered the nation's public
high schools the previous September, only half would remain
till graduation. He proceeded to analyze a study of 1,360

children who had withdrawn voluntarily from public high schools in Ohio, Indiana, and Michigan, which had been conducted by Dr. Harold J. Dillon, Executive Director of the Pennsylvania Public Education and Child Labor Association, for the National Child Labor Committee. There was no evidence that poor family background was influential in their leaving. The number of broken homes represented was not abnormally high, nor was the number of families who had moved from place to place. The parents were typical, average American wage earners.

Certain common factors, however, were observable. There had been a falling off in the students' attendance records for several years before they left. The majority had had to repeat grades, beginning, in 70 per cent of the cases, in the elementary schools. Not more than a quarter of them were engaged in extracurricular activities. Fifty-four per cent left at the age of sixteen; 26 per cent at seventeen; most of them before the end of the second year. Particularly significant of the waste of powers involved is the fact that 40 per cent of the number had intelligence quotients which were normal or better than normal, with nearly a fifth of them above 105.

As for the reasons given for leaving, some said they were not interested in school work and preferred a job; some, that they were failing and did not want to repeat; others, that they disliked a particular teacher or subject, or that they felt they could learn more away from school. There was a general feeling that nobody within the schools was interested in them, that there was no one to whom they could turn for advice.

A third of them held three or more jobs during their first year out of school. About half were sorry they had left.

Studies of public high school mortality rates in other parts of the United States would doubtless arrive at more reassuring findings; yet a rate of 50 per cent for the whole country gives evidence that these are not untypical.

A striking fact about our public high school enrollment is its uneven distribution. In *Education for All American Youth*, published in 1944, prepared by national educational organizations, it was estimated that the number of public high schools after the war would be 28,000 and that, in point of median enrollment, a single school served only 140 students and had six faculty members. The median figures, taken by themselves, would seem to contradict the fact of overcrowding in the schools and lead one to suppose that our educational resources are being spread pretty thin, with plenty to go around. Their real significance is their revelation of the inflexibility of the situation. The population each school serves is fixed in space. It cannot be transferred. Schools which have too many cannot dispatch their overflows to schools which have too few. And since all public high schools are day schools, the imbalance would appear to be insuperable.

But the ability of the public school to offer individualized education, seriously limited already, would seem to be diminished rather than increased by the demands which will be made upon it in the future. Writing in *The American High School*, the eighth yearbook of the John Dewey Society, in 1946, Gordon N. Mackenzie, Professor of Education at Teachers College, Columbia, says, "It appears reasonable to suppose that approximately 90 per cent of the secondary-school-age youth, at least of those under eighteen, will attend school in the next decade. . . . If such a situation should develop, a group would be reached who have been regarded as incapable of doing school work." "This assumes," he remarks, "a program suited to their needs."

With a different sort of need in mind, United States Commissioner of Education Earl J. McGrath has pointed out that about 78 per cent of the nation's fifth-grade students who are mentally qualified for college never get there. Millions of them, he is quoted as saying, "go through life functioning below the level of their potential."

Commissioner McGrath's proposal was the appropriation of three hundred million dollars a year by the federal government to provide college scholarships; the effect of which, inferentially, would be to help only those presently deprived. Meanwhile the President's Commission on Higher Education has called for a doubling of college enrollments by 1960. The obligation to provide equal educational opportunity for all Americans is fundamental. It cannot be blinked. And the President's Commission has plainly faced it. The conclusions it has reached, however, have given rise to some misgivings.

Harvard economist Seymour E. Harris, in his book *The Market for College Graduates*, wonders whether there will be jobs enough of the sort that college graduates have come to expect. The professions, he estimates, which at present attract 65 per cent of college graduates, would find it necessary to provide two or three times as many openings. He sees the consequent possibility that the salary advantage normally enjoyed by college graduates might drop still further. In 1940 college men earned about 32 per cent more than the American average; in 1948 only 10 per cent more. "The time may come," he writes, "when, on the average, the college-trained worker will earn less than the non-college worker."

The merit of these proposals and opinions, the reliability of the estimates on which they are based, and the validity of the inferences derived from them are in some degree matters of opinon. Statistics are notoriously equivocal. Their relevance to the likelihood of improving the quality of education in the public high schools, however, seems clear enough. The additional necessary outlay in plant and personnel will in itself be staggering. And whatever else may happen, the heightened pressure on these schools to accommodate the educational needs of a greatly increased population cannot help, during the foreseeable future, but aggravate their already vexing problems. Through the faith and energy and intelligence of those charged with meeting the problem, progress in solving it is certain to be made. But the progress must seemingly be made along the line of improving the effectiveness of mass education.

Can the public school realistically hope that it can increasingly develop capacities on an individual basis? There is no reason to believe that it can reduce even its present population to comfortable limits, and, once the irresistible expansion has established itself, it is scarcely to be hoped that it will recede. How the public school meets the future is certainly the most important question now facing American education. In the realm of training an aristocracy of brains and character, it is fortunate for the country, and always will be so, that the private school can offer materials and methods—and the freedom to control them—aimed at the improvement of the individual. These are values indispensable to national progress. As such, they are permanent values.

But in its ability to contribute to the cultivation of an aristocratic minority, the public school suffers from further limitations which transcend the problems of outside interference, financial stringencies, and popular apathy.

For the public school, in the first place, cannot select its students. On the whole, it must admit and teach all who wish to attend. To a considerable degree, its curricular offerings must be responsive not only to the needs (as they should be) but to the preferences and the prejudices of its patrons. And since it exists solely for the education of the children of the local taxpayers who support it, its standards and requirements must lie within the capacity of the majority. And these standards and requirements are bound to suffer from the fact that, with notable exceptions, the range of native ability covered by a public school population is extensive.

In its selection of teachers, the public school, against its will and to the detriment of its efficiency, must proceed under hampering limitations. If its controlling body is enlightened, its freedom of choice is adequate for the realization of its purposes; though the ends of education are always better served when teachers are chosen by other teachers, beyond the influence or approval of laymen. Most public school boards and committees, however, are appointed by a political officeholder or elected by the voters. It is proper, of course, that the people should have some measure of control over the educational system for which they pay. They have a right to say, through their representatives, how much teachers shall be paid, if they can get the taxpayers to approve their budget. The trouble comes when political opportunism or personal prejudice blocks the employment of a teacher whom a school wants, or urges and sometimes secures the appointment of someone it does not.

Finally, once a teacher has been engaged, and he or she has fulfilled the number of years of service required by state law for the establishment of "tenure," there the teacher stays till the age of statutory retirement, despite stagnation or obvious incompetence. In purpose, and somewhat ironically, tenure is designed to protect teachers from becoming the pawns of the politics and prejudice that may have had a part in their selection. And in communities where the reshuffling of superintendents, principals, and teachers might normally be expected to follow each change in political administration, there must obviously be the assurance of security in return for faithful, effective work. Tenure, however, should not

become a limb for the support of the lazy, the mentally dead, or the inefficient.

Public schools are a defenseless prey also to fanatical pressure groups with political influence who take it upon themselves to censor textbooks and the free expression of teachers' opinions. Occasionally state legislatures impose compulsory instruction in subjects which the schools themselves consider valueless and a waste of time. Sometimes textbooks are required to be used in certain schools which faculties consider grossly inferior to others which they are forbidden to expound. Respectable and reasonable opinions held by teachers may, if they express them publicly, become the center of protest and contention—and possibly lead to the loss of employment—under the pressure of indignant minorities whose prejudices have been offended. It is the grossest indignity that professionally trained men and women should be made the subjects of such tyranny, and thoughtful people in every community should join arms in stopping it. For as long as it continues, however, the education of the superior can scarcely be attempted, and the education of all the people is maimed and hindered.

CHAPTER III

"*Why the Private School?*"

Despite the superior facilities which the private schools can provide in their context, I think it fair to say that they are widely held, by most people connected with public education, to be insignificant if not contemptible; by the general public, class conscious and snobbish; and, by all but their patrons and proprietors, by definition undemocratic.

It cannot be so merely because of the fact that they are privately financed and, in their standards of admission, selective. For often parents who will not patronize the private school on the ground that it is undemocratic proceed to send their children to such higher institutions as Harvard or Princeton, Smith or Bryn Mawr, Notre Dame or Trinity—all privately financed and all selective in their admissions policies —without any sense that they are acting inconsistently. The responsive argument is frequently that the endowed colleges and universities become, in some fashion, "democratic" because they are "national." Some of them are national. So are some of the private schools; which is to say that the argument is not in fact responsive at all. What, then, is the basis for the common attitude toward the private school? And what are the facts from which the attitude is derived?

These are questions which call, at this point, for some discussion of the position of the private school in America yesterday and today: for an appraisal of its assets and its liabilities, its strengths and its weaknesses; for an examination of the intellectual, social, political, and economic climate within which it must operate. That climate is radically different from what it used to be. It contains elements which seem to many to threaten the very survival of the private school. Others, recognizing the same elements, regard them as opportunities. There is need for an attempt to balance the factors that affect the private school's performance of that function in a program of democratic education which it seems to be especially equipped to serve.

To some students of American education the most striking feature of the private school has been its discontinuity of purpose, its failure to establish and hold firmly to a single, consistent role throughout its long history. They point out that the earliest American private school—the Latin grammar school—limited itself to the training of an exclusive minority for the ministry and other learned professions; that it was imported, not indigenous; and that when the social, political, and economic conditions faced by the colonists became radically different from those in the mother country, these transplanted schools, designed to serve a tradition now grown obsolete, died.

That, of course, is precisely what happened. But the old New England academy, established in the late eighteenth and early nineteenth centuries, and its prototypes in other parts of the country were native American schools. They were the people's schools. They cut themselves free from the narrow classical curriculum and preprofessional emphasis of the early grammar schools and gave the people the sort of variety and freedom of choice that they felt would meet their real needs and interests. By 1850 over six thousand academies were in operation, with a student population of a quarter of a million.

The academy movement greatly increased the numbers whose educational needs were met under private auspices. But it has always been true, and always must and should be true, that the private school is for the few rather than the many. It must be so by reason of financial limitations. It should be so because its service to the country stipulates a high degree of selectivity. With the rise of the public school, therefore, beginning in the 1830's, the academy largely disappeared, and its few relatively ancient survivors have changed substantially in both function and objectives.

But the absence of continuity that these metamorphoses suggest is far less significant than the extraordinary adaptability to changing opportunities that the private school has throughout its history exhibited. Being free to serve as it thought best, it has repeatedly and flexibly responded to new conditions and entered new fields of usefulness. The virtual extinction of the American academy, therefore, far from sounding the death knell of the private school, ushered in a period in which private schools expanded, in both numbers and influence, beyond precedent or expectation.

The present American private school, typically if not always chronologically, sprang up after the Civil War. Whereas the academy had represented terminal education to a considerable number of its students and had provided practical as well as cultural instruction, the private school during the past seventy-five or eighty years has become almost entirely a college preparatory school. The period between the Civil War and the depression introduced by the stock market collapse of 1929 was one of extraordinary economic expansion. National income increased rapidly, particularly in the case of businessmen and industrialists, who came to constitute a new American middle and upper-middle class. They began to send their children to private schools.

Those of us who have been connected with boys' schools, particularly the older boarding schools, find our ears continuously assailed by tales of the glories of the eighties and nineties, when men were giants who later, by some monstrous perversity of nature, sired a generation of effete dilettantes. The giants generally attribute the fault to the schools. But they are talking about something which has real importance in the history of private education, and which it is vitally important for the private schools to realize as they face the future. During the last two decades of the nineteenth century the atmosphere of such schools was one of "rugged individualism." The sons of the new rich were often rough diamonds, and the life they led at school was a process of attrition in which survival, not to speak of supremacy, required physical stamina, mental fiber, and social resilience. Teachers were natural enemies of boys, stern and forbidding taskmasters, whose underlying compassion was infrequently exhibited and almost never conceded by the young. Without the relative luxuries of modern physical equipment, and with "individual attention" not only untried but held in cordial disrepute as "mollycoddling," life was a struggle in which victory was always hard won and therefore memorably sweet. I have the impression, which I cannot prove, that a disproportionately large number of the graduates of such schools who won distinction in later life have been the product of those times.

One of the reasons was that the schools set high standards and enforced them rigorously and relentlessly. But the underlying cause was that the times were characterized by the optimism of a rapidly expanding economy and by the conviction of permanent economic security. Private enterprise was in its heyday, and there lay before the boys the inviting and exhilarating prospect of unlimited rewards for individual initiative and competitive energy, of ultimate success in a hard and exciting fight. The world was their oyster, and they knew it always would be.

Well, it isn't any more, and the change is one which the private schools must take to heart. The security is gone. Estate and income taxes are making inroads upon accumulations of wealth. The income group that has largely supported the private school for the past century is no longer sure of itself. It feels itself to be under attack. It is bitter, frustrated, and fearful. The rise of the "welfare state" has thrown its whole set of values out of gear. Children in private schools today reflect the apprehensions and anxieties of their parents. To prepare them for the sort of world they will live in as adults, such schools must search their hearts and minds as they have never done before. Nostalgic lamentation is inappropriate. However good the good old days may have been, they are lost forever. It is the future that tests us.

The prospect, however, should not be fearful or disheartening to men and women of intelligence, humility, and faith. Private schools have reached the end of a phase. But they have done that repeatedly before and found for themselves new strength and greater usefulness. The best of them, indeed, have been going about their business, through a variety of alarums and excursions, for a good many years. They are certain to continue to do so.

In clarifying its present situation, however, the private school would do well to examine some of the popular attitudes to which it is currently subject. Many people on the eastern seaboard, for example, are inclined to take the private secondary school for granted. The New England colonies were the birthplace of American private education, and even today that area contains a concentration of private schools quite disproportionate to its total population. Institutions similar in kind were gradually established throughout the Middle Atlantic states and southward. But the movement lost momentum as it turned west. A majority of the graduates of private boarding schools live in the East, most of them in or near large cities. They do not always realize that the vogue of private education tapers off steadily to the west, or that the public attitude toward it, in large areas of the country, amounts not so much to opposition as to indifference. In those districts it is hard to find a private school of high quality. It is hard to find good public high schools too, or much if any interest in educational standards. Good schools, whether public or private, flourish only where there is persistent popular demand for them. Even where quality is not the issue, however, millions of Americans believe that the value of private education is negligible, and their support of public schools and particularly local schools is a deeply rooted tradition.

In the light of this attitude, the question, "Why the private school at all?" must be recognized as being a real one in many people's minds. Education for everyone, they say, is provided at public expense. Private schools represent a duplication of facilities and effort. They limit their attention to only a small fraction of the school population. The money spent on them could better be directed toward the improvement and expansion of public education. Why the private school at all?

The answer is first of all perhaps the repetition of a question already suggested: How concerned are we Americans that our schools shall provide for the full development of every child's capacities? Education for all we do supply. But though it is an impressive accomplishment, it does not meet the question. It has nothing to say of the value of what is being offered. It does not preclude a concern for individual potentialities, to be sure; but also it does not stipulate it, to say nothing of guaranteeing it. And it is clearly possible to offer a service to everybody which may fall far short, in point of real worth, of the representations made in its behalf or of the hopes entertained for it.

In view of the conditions under which public education in America must now proceed, there would seem to be little to support the argument that the private school as an American institution is useless and moribund. The identification and training of boys and girls of superior intelligence and character are of critical importance in a program of democratic education. It cannot be argued that private schools are unnecessary in the discharge of this function because the public schools are already covering it adequately. They are not, and on the face of it they cannot. If private schools do not meet the need, then it simply cannot be met. There is plenty of room for the contention that they are not meeting it as well as they should, as there is for the opinion that public schools too fall short of delivering what they promise. But the discovery that an important role is sometimes being poorly played surely suggests its improvement, not its elimination.

An extensive reading of published criticisms leveled against the value of the private school reveals a disturbing and unhealthy misconception of its claims and an ignorance of its methods. At times, of course, the claims it makes for its own importance are overweening, rhetorical, and absurd. Occasionally, for example, private schools represent themselves as bustling laboratories of educational experiment, in which men and women, with sacerdotal zeal, are forever blazing new trails which public schools may follow. This is a delusion of grandeur. There is much of value that private schools can do.

But they cannot hope to exert significant influence upon the great group of public schools. Thoughtful private school people, however, would assert, firmly but more moderately, that their purpose was to instill in men and women certain specific qualities of mind and spirit likely, in their opinion, to exert, through the influence of example, an elevating effect on American life. Since it is a fact that some private schools do this well, it is a pity that so many of their critics write and talk as if they either were unaware of it or thought it unimportant. The private school regards its functions as consistent with and supplementary to the function of public education. It does not hold that the two functions are the same or that the private school duplicates the work of the public school. It does not think that one kind of school is better than the other. It applauds diversity in schools. It deplores the ignorance and misunderstanding that separate workers in the private and public schools, making them seem to some to operate in different worlds. It regrets the acerbity, the recriminations, the occasional venom that ignorance and misunderstanding have called forth from both groups. It feels the necessity of unity, of a sense of partnership in a great profession. And naturally it feels impelled to raise its voice when things are said about it that are not so.

One of the things being said about it today is that it cannot justify its privateness; an attitude which suggests the usefulness of dissolving some popular misconceptions.

The general charge is that the private school cannot be justified because it is not democratic. At this point a distinction needs to be made, because two different matters are involved. One is whether any school conducted under private auspices is for that reason and by definition undemocratic. The other is whether the charge is brought against such schools not as a point of principle but because their administration is characteristically marked by undemocratic practices.

As to the first question, the word "private" as attached to certain schools would seem to be, as a term of definition and distinction, simple, accurate, and inoffensive. On the subject of democracy or the lack of it it is silent. It contains no political connotations, and none may fairly be read into it. "Private" is merely the opposite of "public." It identifies institutions whose expenses are met from "private" sources, as distinguished from other institutions which are financed by taxing the "public." In the first instance, support comes voluntarily from individuals who are exercising their right to provide for their children the sort of education they prefer. In the second instance, support comes from every taxpayer by compulsion. The American commitment that education for everybody should be provided at "public" expense is a national responsibility. The proposition that Americans are free to maintain, in addition, other schools conducted under "private" auspices, if they wish to do so, is equally a part of our democratic tradition.

Yet this freedom, though it is embedded in our political philosophy, is under wide attack today as a repudiation of it. Being disposed to clarify the popular confusion and relieve emotional tension, the private schools have largely abandoned the word "private," which they take to be misleading and therefore suggestive of unjustifiable interpretations, and have adopted, in the title of their national organization, the word "independent," which more accurately describes their status. But to the more vocal and indignant champions of sundry private versions of democratic theory, the new word has not had the effect of making the rose smell sweeter. To the extremist an educational institution whose facilities are not placed at the disposal of everyone who wants them is discriminatory and subject to condemnation.

In an article in *School and Society* for March 12, 1949, entitled "Is the Private School Antidemocratic?" Dean J. Leonard Sherman of the Harvard School in North Hollywood, California, writes: "When . . . the private school can better perform a given educational function than can a public school, every private school is in duty bound by democratic society to make that educational advantage available to all who can intellectually profit by that opportunity."

Dean Sherman's viewpoint is not consistent with American ideals. Throughout our life as a nation one of our most highly prized rights has been the freedom of the individual to improve his lot, by his own initiative and effort, so that he could provide himself and his family with goods and services which he considered superior, if he could afford to buy them. Any abridgment of this freedom would be a limitation of democracy as we understand it.

A service which is available to everyone on the same terms is obviously democratic; but it is necessary to abandon logic and common sense to maintain that other services which are available only at a price are for that reason undemocratic and therefore worthy of public censure. Given adequate means and an optional choice, a man will patronize a free public medical clinic not because it is democratic, but only because it offers a service better than his purse can buy. Without the means, his selection of the free clinic expresses not public spirit but necessity.

It is sound American doctrine that a man is similarly free to choose whatever school he pleases for his children and for whatever reason, regardless of whether his reason seems good or bad to anybody else, or whether he prefers a good school or a bad one. It is essential to our purposes as a nation to preserve that freedom; to see to it that in a democracy men and women with ideas on the subject of education shall be free to organize them in a corporate project, just as they may in any other field of endeavor. If their ideas are abortive, if they do not take root, their projects will fail, and it is natural and proper that they should. Freedom to launch them, however, is so vitally important that it is the only justification needed for the right of the private school to exist in a democratic state.

If, on the other hand, the charge that the private school is undemocratic is brought because its administration is considered to be marked by undemocratic practices, discussion of the question must shift its ground. It is true that private schools are in peculiar danger of adopting undemocratic practices, and that many of them do. Their freedom to select both teachers and pupils includes a freedom to discriminate and segregate if they are pleased or tempted to do so. If they yield at this point, they merit censure, on grounds not only of practice but of principle. For their privileges impose responsibilities which they may not in good conscience abrogate.

But the absolution of their sins ought to be just that: a matter of conscience rather than compulsion. And it is perfectly safe for the democracy to let it go at that. For in the private school adherence to undemocratic practices will in the long run prove to be a form of suicide—lingering, perhaps, but certain to result in extinction. Meanwhile the best such schools are devoted to their mission of making better men and women. They are using their freedom to set standards which no honest judge would assert were exceeded elsewhere. Most important of all, they are acutely aware of their responsibilities, and they are working with intelligence and consecration to perfect themselves as agencies of democratic education—as only private schools are free to do.

Much of the controversy against the justification of the private school uses abstract nouns loosely. It uses them as slogans, which lack intellectual precision because they are intended to incite rather than enlighten. They contain a heavy emotional content which throws up a smoke screen against clear thinking. A critic contrives a definition of when a school is democratic and when it is not. He decides (he does not discover) that a school is democratic when it is a public school and undemocratic when it is private. This may pass for logical thought in some circles. To others it suggests prejudice rather than proof. It ignores the obvious fact that it is possible for a given private school to be intensely democratic and a given public school to be ridden by intolerance and snobbery. By inference it gives a sort of plenary blessing to enterprises under public auspices. It permits the conclusion that a poor public school is more democratic than a good private school, a view which I should suppose would give comfort to no one. It leaves quality as a factor in democratic education out of the picture.

Now, that is not a reasonable thing to do. If it is impossible to indict a people for the crimes of individuals, it is impossible to consign to perdition all private education because some of its practitioners are culpable and feeble. When Dean Sherman, in the article previously cited, writes that "The evolution in American education left to the private secondary school the role of being a mere adjunct to the system by catering either to that favored economic group that could afford to pay for an education fostered and nurtured in an exclusive environment or to . . . denominational folds," it seems to me that he is doing exactly that. He is applying to all private schools, good and bad, the undeniable faults of the worst. And in so doing, he is using a number of emotional words whose connotation is derogatory.

Dr. Arthur E. Traxler, Executive Director of the Educational Records Bureau, writing on *The Independent School and Education, Yesterday, Today, and Tomorrow,* in *School and Society* for November 28, 1942, says,

Although in recent years not more than one boy in a hundred has been educated in the private schools of the United States, these schools have, according to information contained in *Who's Who in America*, educated approximately as many leaders as all the public schools combined. It seems probable that the generally superior environment which it affords for its pupils is the greatest single strength of the independent school and that it largely explains the survival of this type of school long after excellent public schools were established throughout the nation.

Dr. Traxler's comment restores a balance. Admittedly, however, no case can be proved by the citation of opinions, however attractive they may seem to school debaters.

Schools can justify themselves only by the soundness of their standards and the degree to which they realize them. A just appraisal of a school must begin, therefore, with a consideration of its stated objectives and, with these firmly in mind, continue toward a judgment of how fully they are being accomplished. This is the method followed by the evaluating committees of the various regional Associations of Colleges and Secondary Schools, which hold entirely reasonably that a school may not fairly be called deficient for failing to espouse objectives which it has no wish to serve. A school whose purposes are commendable, but whose standards of performance are lax, is a poor school. It is selling its patrons short; and the damage it does within the limits of its influence is not alleviated though its student population represent an unrestricted cross section of the people. Nor can its shortcomings be tolerated when their effect is confined to a wealthy few. It is simply a bad school, and there is no excuse for it.

This fact ought to be kept in mind in any discussion of the question When is a school democratic? Of the public schools, for example, it is not enough to point out that they take children of all creeds, races, colors, economic and social groups, mix them up together, and make them rub shoulders with each other. This is of course a democratic thing to do. It provides a setting in which democratic education may well take place and which private schools cannot provide. Public schools have produced in our national "melting pot" millions of loyal Americans from the most diverse social and intellectual ingredients. It has been a magnificent achievement. But there is more to democratic education than that. The stated objective of American public education is to offer to every individual an opportunity for the full development of his capacities. The objective is *achieved* only when the capacities are in fact fully developed. In some public schools the objective is substantially realized. In others it is realized imperfectly or barely approached. It is this, rather than merely the practice of a nondiscriminatory admissions policy, which determines not, to be sure, whether a public school may be certified as democratic, but whether, in the actual advancement of national educational purposes, it is really any good or not.

These observations apply with equal force to the private schools. Their stated objectives are on a high level and are consonant with American democratic ideals. Like the public schools, they have had a hand in the training of large numbers of effective citizens and notable leaders; and the best of them, like the best of the public schools, have succeeded in developing the full capacities of their students. Measured by the service they have evidently rendered to the education of Americans, some of them come out with a high rating, and the most biased critic would scarcely suggest that theirs has not been a real contribution to the strength and the quality of the democracy. Surely, then, the contribution itself is not less valuable because it has been made through the few rather than the many. Obviously the opportunities for development presented by the private schools would be vastly more influential in American life if more people could have access to them. Nobody believes that more firmly than the private schools themselves. But it would be a gross lapse of judgment to suppose that the intrinsic value of their work has any conceivable relationship to the numbers who benefit from it. The value is undiminished. Its influence is simply more limited than it ought to be.

So much for the good private schools. As for the rest, they are vulnerable to criticism not because they are private but because they are bad; because examination reveals that they are not living up to their pretensions; just as some public schools are bad for the same reason. They may both be judged because their product does not measure up to specifications. Bad schools are an extravagance which the country cannot afford; and it makes no difference whether they are public or private schools. A definition of democratic education which does not match purpose against performance is scarcely adequate to the country's needs.

Freedom of access, therefore, is not by any means the only test of a school's democracy. It must be measured also by the degree to which democratic principles and practices prevail in the life of the school. I have said that the diversity of backgrounds from which the public schools draw provides a setting in which democratic education may well take place. It does not guarantee that it will. Democracy is a spirit, an ideal. It expresses itself in a way of living. If those responsible for the management of a school are stirred by the ideal and devoted to its exercise, they are likely to develop a dem-

ocratic atmosphere. It ought to surprise no one that this
atmosphere has been secured at times in private schools as
well as public, or that, in other instances, both types of schools
have fallen short. For the enemies of democracy are hatred
and prejudice and ignorance and fear and greed; and these
unlovely passions are inherent not in institutions but in men
and women. Diversity of race and color and creed, therefore, does not itself imply, or even make more likely, freedom
from their disruptive influence. Fascism, communism, Ku-
Kluxism, Jew-baiting, and Jim Crowism are no respecters of
persons, but afflict indiscriminately the educated population,
without reference to the sort of school they attend.

In consequence, there is no basis for the generalization that
the way of life in public schools is intrinsically more democratic than that in private schools. The degree of democracy differs among individual schools, not between kinds of
schools. You can find private schools in which members of
any race or creed are accepted unreservedly on their individual merits; and public school districts, in the North as
well as the South, in which Negroes are segregated. A Jew,
coming to a private boarding school for a year after his
graduation from a large metropolitan public high school, is
elected, in competition with Gentiles, to the presidency of his
house for the last half-year. He declares that the year has
been the first in his life in which he has felt perfectly free
from anti-Semitic prejudice; and that the office to which he
has been elected would have been hopelessly out of his reach
in his high school because of his race, which had also kept
him out of a high school fraternity.

A private school headmaster is told by boys who came to
it from public schools that they "relish the democratic atmosphere . . . in contrast to the lack of it in the high schools
from which [they] have come, where considerations of

wealth, as expressed by cars and clothes and the position that
one's father holds, seem to classify boys and girls in a more
rigid caste system than seems to obtain in a school of this
kind."

On the other hand, you have the private school boy who
says he would resign if a Negro were admitted and another,
from a wealthy background, who is an incorrigible snob; and
a private school which let it be known at one time that no
Jews need apply. In the face of such extreme disparities, the
facts will sustain no generalizations whatsoever, for the
practice is as various as human nature and as unpredictable.

If any school, therefore, hopes to offer not merely equality
of opportunity but a scheme of life firmly based on democratic practices, it must meet certain stipulations. It must be
open, of course, to every qualified person who wants to attend
it. Its course of study must be responsive to the needs,
purposes, and capabilities of its students, and it must recognize
its obligation to enhance their moral stature as well as to
endow them with skills. Whatever the content of the curriculum, the standard of accomplishment must provide a rigorous test of the powers of its students. The school must
establish a system under which the full extension of individual ability is possible. And its social atmosphere must
reflect respect for personality on grounds of merit only.

This is a tall order, but it is also a clear one. Granted the
probability that no school can perfectly fill it, it furnishes a
formula by which a school can gauge its real effectiveness in
meeting the demands properly made upon it. Fortunately
there are public and private schools which notably exemplify
it. They encourage the hope that American education may
some day become not only universal but also genuinely democratic.

The most vigorous attacks on the private school often

betray ignorance about its organization. It is commonly supposed and frequently implied, for example, that a "private" school is a school conducted under private ownership for private profit. Though such schools do exist, they are a small minority of the whole group, and their number is decreasing. In such a school the proprietor might conceivably be under a peculiar temptation to give the customers what they wanted, as any other business does, in order to make money; and he might be disposed to cultivate the well-to-do. It is extraordinarily unlikely, however, that the well-to-do would continue to cultivate him if he ran a poor school. And the hypothesis itself is by no means inescapable, for there have been and are proprietary schools of the highest grade which have rendered a valuable educational service. Futhermore, a school conducted for profit is taxed like any other business and so pays its share toward the support of public enterprises in its community.

Occasionally private schools have been guilty of subterfuges designed to make them appear to be nonprofit institutions when they were not; but the law can deal with dishonesty and trickery wherever they are proved, and a rascal is a rascal whatever his line of work.

But by far the greater and a steadily increasing number of private schools, whether they be day or boarding schools, are chartered by the state as educational corporations not for profit. That is to say that they are licensed by the public under the terms of public law. In giving sanction to them the people are exercising rather than relinquishing their democratic rights. Such chartered schools must meet the requirements of state statutes, and therefore they carry a specified public responsibility. Their ownership is vested not in individuals but in a board of trustees, whose number and qualifications are described in the charter and who bear a precisely stated legal obligation in their operation of the school. Any substantive changes in their organization must be sanctioned by the proper state authorities. If such a school has an operating surplus, it must by law be applied to school purposes, and none of it can accrue to the benefit, let alone the profit, of any individual.

In considering the financial support of American schools, it is worth noticing here that our public schools are "free" only in the special sense that they are open to everyone. They are not free in the sense that they educate the people without cost. Every taxpayer contributes to their support. Patrons of private schools are also paying school taxes in their home communities, a charge for services not received. They are providing for the education of their children at public expense and at the same time relieving the public schools of the cost of teaching them. The saving is evidently considerable.

If it meets all legal requirements, a private school operating under a corporate charter is sometimes given a measure of tax exemption on buildings and real estate used for educational purposes, the rest of its property being taxed at the same rate imposed on individual ownership. In some states such a school pays no taxes. Occasionally tax-free schools make voluntary contributions to the public income. Hostile critics are apt to talk as if tax-free independent schools owe their status to some sort of chicanery which they themselves have initiated. The fact is that the tax position of a private school is always prescribed by state law and never arrived at by connivance. If the communities in which private schools operate feel that they are being deprived, by reason of tax exemption, of income which is rightly theirs, they are free to apply to the courts for a judgment on the situation under the stipulations of the law; and if they do not like the law, they can press for its revision. The private school itself should not be made a scapegoat. To an institution sanctioned by state license and subject to the stipulations of state law, the usual connotations of the word "private" are inappropriate.

As for taxing the "profits" of private schools, if they are nonprofit corporations there are obviously no profits. Many of the best of them charge a fee which is less than cost, counting on income from endowment and on annual giving to meet deficits. In such schools every student has a partial scholarship. During the postwar years inflationary prices have brought about in a good many private schools an annual operating deficit, which has had to be absorbed by such surplus as may have been accumulated in the past; and when there have been modest surpluses, they have generally been swallowed up by capital expenses for which no other funds were available; or, again, have been laid aside against the contingency of future deficits. In the absence of profits, therefore, if incorporated private schools were to be taxed on their occasional operating surplus, the effect would be not so much to swell the public coffers as to put the schools out of business.

CHAPTER IV

Failures and Fallings-short

When the uncertain tax status of the private school is set against its increasing operating expense and the rising income taxes laid upon its would-be patrons, its most serious single limitation is brought into sharp focus: the independent schools cost too much. The boarding school group is, for all but a minority of American families, prohibitively expensive. And even the private day school comes high to parents of modest income who are called upon also to pay taxes for the support of local public schools. To a regrettable extent, that is to say, the private schools cannot be run on a quality basis: they must be run on a price basis. They cannot confine their student groups to the best boys and girls in point of desire and fitness for the kind of education they want to offer. They are obliged, in varying degree, to take the best boys and girls there are who can pay the price.

It is encouraging that so many who can pay the price are worth everything they get for it. But the ranks of the private schools contain far too many young people who are admitted chiefly because they *can* pay the price; whose intrinsic qualities do not by the most charitable of standards mark them out as superior. It is fortunate, too, that most private schools can offer scholarships to promising students who cannot pay the price, but that can go only so far. These institutions, as I am frequently reminded by my business office, must pay their bills or go out of business. And the presence of some scholarship holders merely highlights the predicament of thousands of other able youths who cannot choose the kind of education they want and ought to get because there is no means of paying for it.

It is the presence in our private schools of so many children admitted on a price basis which, in the words of Frank D. Ashburn, headmaster of Brooks School, "greatly increases the chances of silverspoonitis, that debilitating disease, congenital, which makes boys take much for granted, which, if they were less fortunate (or unfortunate), they would realize was a remarkable privilege." Now, "silverspoonitis" is an affliction with which the American people will have no truck; and they are quite right about it. It is hard, too, for the schools themselves to bear; and they are only human when they complain at being blamed for a predicament which they cannot prevent and from which they can be rescued only by the provision of sums of money so large as to be, to many of them, unprocurable.

The predicament of the privately endowed colleges and universities is comparable, but with a difference. As the schools need money to *bring* their price down, the higher institutions need it, and many times more of it, to *keep* it down. It is because their price is already relatively low, and therefore within the means of a broad range of annual incomes, that the general public considers them more "democratic" than the private schools; as in that sense (and a very important sense it is) they are.

In short, the private schools cannot at present offer equality of opportunity, and to the extent that they cannot, they are limited in the fulfillment of their proper function. This is a matter of acute concern to responsible private school teachers. Many people speak as if they think that the preponderance of the rather well-to-do in such institutions denotes a positive preference for them, an assiduous cultivation of them, a deliberate attempt to attract them, on the part of the schools themselves—on the ground that they *want* to be class schools. The opposite is true. I know no head of a good private school who would not feel that his most pressing problem had been solved if he could admit *all* students on the basis of capacity rather than of ability to pay.

The remedy for this situation is of course financial, and it can be accomplished only by bringing to the assistance of private school students very large sums of money. In consequence the private schools must appeal to their patrons and to their graduates for increasing annual support as well as for capital gifts and bequests. The endowed colleges and universities have been doing just that with energy, systematic organization, and increasing momentum and success for many years. More recently the private schools have followed their example, and they must continue to do so. Those who believe that the private school has an indispensable role to perform in American education must repeatedly be called upon to support their faith. The ground of the appeal, to be honest and worthy of respect, must be the support of real educational values, not an invitation to alleviate a given school's competitive physical inadequacies, and certainly not a shameless titillation of the emotions of sentiment, affection, or "school spirit." The objective must be a double one: money to effectuate equality of opportunity for able students, who are the school's chief concern; and money for the adequate remuneration and security of teachers. The private school that clearly sees its function and performs it with power will in my opinion get the material support it deserves. But if it simply takes mediocrity and the commonplace as its goal, and achieves them, it had better shut up shop.

But the solicitation of private benefactions by individual schools, even if it proves successful, has grave limitations. At best it can secure the solvency and broaden the opportunities of the particular institutions whose supporters are most responsive and most liberal. But all the money so received by all the private schools can barely scratch the surface of the nation's need for equality of educational opportunity for the ablest individuals. Such a program has the further disadvantage that its support must come from a group whose freedom to give is becoming progressively more limited by reason of the tax situation.

If it is agreed that the independent school has a national function to perform, and if it seems desirable to develop it to the full so that it may include a substantial proportion of the nation's ablest youth—or at least be made available to those of them who want it—it seems essential that federal scholarships be provided to support its program. I am aware of the standard arguments against federal aid to private education: That those who invest money in an enterprise, whether they be individuals or governments, but particularly if they be governments, feel a natural and irresistible impulse to have a say in how the money is spent, in how the enterprise is managed. It is generally felt also that politicians, in the interests of their re-election, would scramble with each other for larger shares of federal bounty. I share these apprehensions. Furthermore, I firmly believe that if the private schools are to do their full part in American education, they must remain absolutely free to do the kind of work they believe in and to do it in the way that seems to them best.

But I am not talking about federal aid to schools. I am

talking about federal aid to individuals. The country is already divided into regional associations of colleges and secondary schools which are supported by both public and private institutions. These are accrediting organizations. They set the standard that schools and colleges in their district must meet in order to be accredited. They have no jurisdiction over the institutions that compose them. They have no favors to bestow or withhold; no money at their disposal; no ax to grind. Their only function is to set standards for membership; if schools or colleges do not meet the standards, all the associations can do about it is to deny them membership, which has a bad effect on the professional reputation of those which are rejected.

I think it feasible to suggest that these regional associations devise and administer competitive scholarship examinations within their districts to all who care to present themselves; that the winners be free to choose the school or college they wish to enter, wherever it may be; that the amount of the scholarship be paid to the winners, from whom evidence should be required that the money is actually spent to defray educational expenses; or, alternatively, that the money be paid to the institution selected, in the name of the winner; and finally that the costs be met by federal funds.

It is quite possible that there are in this plan elements or implications which would threaten free institutions of learning, though I have not been able to discover them. Certainly I should greatly prefer that nation-wide equality of educational opportunity at the higher levels of ability be made possible from private sources, at least as far as the private institutions are concerned. But I do not, even by the wildest extension of optimism, believe it can be done. And opportunity must be broadly increased if the ends envisioned by American education are to be fully realized.

I look forward to an educational establishment so fluid and so free that youth of exceptional capacity could move about in it as their needs directed. The mere statement of such a utopia may sound sentimental and fuzzyheaded. But the point, as I see it, is not that we are far, far short of it. It is that in our present formlessness and lack of plan we are not even moving toward it.

I am dealing here, of course, with private schools in general, for the problem of financial stringency is common to all of them. Except for such specific matters, however, it is misleading, if not impossible, to talk about private schools "in general," because they vary so widely in substance and in quality. Anyone who really knows the best of the private schools, both day and boarding, would be bound to admit that the work they do is first class, whether or not he approved of them in theory. But, nationally speaking, it is true beyond question that there are many more second- and third-rate schools than there are first-class ones; and this fact further colors the public reputation of them all.

Of some private schools—and my guess is that there are more of them than I know of personally—it may be said without irony that the most impressive thing about them is their catalogues. Anyone who has read extensively what private schools say about themselves in their own publications must have felt, as I have, that he was entering a roseate world of peaceful utopias, in which the language used is vague, general, swooningly edifying, and unrelievedly high minded, and every campus an academic Eden—before the Fall. The institutions I have worked for, on the other hand, have been not only antedated, but apparently anticipated, by the Fall, and have been clearly rich in its consequences. My own research in this field, as well as my occasional contributions to its literature, has led me to the rueful recognition that, sty-

listically speaking, the school catalogue performs a painful
disservice to the cause of private education.

And sometimes the pretensions of some of the schools are
incredible. Here is a school which "integrates college preparation with training for citizenship and world co-operation"—
an ordeal, I should suppose, requiring exceptional stamina. It
has "enriched" courses too. Here are some tall orders culled
from advertisements: "specialized leadership training"; "building character"; "rapid progress assured"; "friendly masters";
"educates the whole boy"; "beautiful campus"; "magnificent
equipment"; "two gymnasiums." Some schools call attention
to the number of miles by motor separating them from the
nearest large cities, thus emphasizing their convenient accessibility, and implying also that their patrons would naturally
eschew the common carriers. Many schools are reassuring on
the subject of remedial reading. A few declare their exceptional skill in meeting the needs of children who are carefully
described as "normal," but who require specially individualized instruction.

Were nothing more important involved, it would be merely
a matter of curiosity and of mild entertainment to discover
what it is such schools think they must offer in order to "sell"
themselves, competitively speaking, to prospective patrons.
Too often it is the trivia: buildings and equipment, beauty of
setting; or an appeal to privilege and to exclusiveness based
on material superiority. And it is common and painful knowledge to any private school head that, to many parents, these
are precisely the things that do count. In part, they constitute
the snob appeal, an ill to which all private schools are heir,
but from which the inferior school protests its immunity
through the simple expedient of calling the disease by some
less ignominious name. It is these run-of-the-mill institutions
which are responsible for the opinion, widely held in America,

that the private school is typically a place for the problem child, the delinquent, or the snob, rather than a place where the pursit of excellence and high standards may be found; that only those who don't get along, who need special this and that, whose homes are not what they should be, go to private schools. In consequence, as Principal William A. Saltonstall of the Phillips Exeter Academy has said, "One cannot travel far abroad without finding evidence of the most abysmal ignorance of private schools and their aims and practices."

Quite recently, a group of private school men in the East became convinced of the necessity of an effective means through which the real purposes and the broad functions of such schools could be communicated. They aimed not merely at "educating the public" in the interests of a wider patronage; but, much more important, at clarifying and encouraging, in co-operation with the public educational authorities, the distinctive contributions that each kind of school could make. They have therefore instituted the National Council of Independent Schools, which, during the short time it has been in existence, has given strong leadership and clear direction to the cause it serves.

There is some reason to hope that the ranks of second- or third-rate private schools will be depleted by the slow process of economic attrition. That is to say, as the high cost of private education tends to limit the number of American families who want and can afford to patronize it, there will evidently, at least for some time to come, be fewer candidates to go around, with the result that some schools will necessarily fall by the wayside. In fact, since the end of World War II, that is exactly what has happened in a surprisingly large number of cases. In this respect it seems probable that the boarding school will suffer more than the day school. The serious and regrettable consequence is that, by reason of financial stringency due to lack of patronage, some good schools may go which very much deserve to survive, while others will survive whose influence on the cause of American education is damaging.

The stock-market crash of 1929 and the ensuing depression hit the private schools in the early thirties. The next dozen years do not constitute, I fear, the most edifying chapter in the history of these institutions. Being one of them myself, I am keenly aware of the anxiety that weighed then upon heads of schools, who were responsible for their financial solvency and accountable to boards of trustees. Many schools kept a sensitive ear cocked in the direction of public sentiment. Visitors to their campuses were given a reception so cordial as to approach, if not to overreach, effusiveness. They became adept at the breaking down of "sales resistance" —always in a nice way, of course. Though times were hard, they were scarcely able to say so about themselves, and the rationalizations they devised to justify their cheerfulness were ingenious and diverting. It was a competitive struggle, and some of them did some things which, though they did try to "follow the gleam," suggested that they attached to its meaning a connotation different from the one which Tennyson had in mind.

Some schools cut prices and outbid each other, though they did not call it that. A father said to me, "School X will take my two boys for Y dollars apiece. What will you offer?" Parents "shopped around." They made deals. Repeatedly during those years parents asked me for a reduction in tuition; and, when they were given an application blank requiring them to state their income, lost interest and went on their way. "Scholarships," intended for students of ability who could not pay the full charge, were given to candidates who did not warrant it by reason of their capabilities. Capacity to pay became a principal academic asset, and the ranks of many private schools were recruited in part from marginal or sub-marginal candidates. The instruction of the unfit placed extra burdens upon teachers. As far as college preparation was concerned, the volume of applications had waned at that level too, selectivity was limited, and the mediocre often got in. The whole episode was bad for standards and did the reputation of the private school no good.

I do not recall it for the sake of admonishing the schools, though the worst offenders probably deserve it. I suspect that there were few, if any, which did not give way at some point at least a little; which did not in some measure feel the pinch of the economic shoe; and for many of the others survival seemed to be at stake. I mention it because the lowering of standards digs a ditch from which it is hard for any school to climb out; because lowered sights are hard to raise; and because their effects are present in the schools today, obscuring their vision of their mission.

My conclusions in this respect are offered with as much of humility and understanding as I can summon to sustain me. None of us in whose hands rests the ultimate responsibility for the motives and the direction of a private school can escape participation in the chorus of *mea culpa* in which his professional commitments involve him. But it is profoundly disturbing to observe how many of us, not seeing the woods for the trees, seem to be preoccupied with the material concerns of our little worlds, sometimes, apparently, to the gross neglect of our zeal for the quality of our schools as instruments of education.

When we are called upon to consider our limitations, we are so likely to forget that it is ourselves that we appraise. We are so prone to say—and to feel—that all that separates us from the consummation of our mission, all that comprises our failures and our fallings-short, is the lack of such useful but inconsequential assets as facilities for winter sports, or more space for science, or endowment for new buildings, or library or auditorium or classroom expansion. Sometimes our emphasis on the material seems endlessly repetitive and almost obsessive.

Such blindness in us is appalling and dangerous. At a time when American education is crying for quality, for the repudiation of the dominance of mediocrity, it is difficult to see how some of our private schools can expect to be taken seriously by those in search of the best that can be found. Fortunately there are other private schools whose perception of what is needed is so clear, and whose humility is so sincere, that they are full of hope and promise.

As for the widely held opinion that the private school is socially exclusive, there is damaging evidence in support of it. I do not mean the sort of exclusiveness that favors the well-to-do. That emphasis is unfortunate and regrettable, but it springs, as I have shown, from the necessity of private schools to meet their costs. I mean the sort of exclusiveness that has prompted the private schools, by and large, to discriminate among their applicants on grounds of race, color, religion, or social or economic background. The motivating force is sometimes snobbery—the conviction held by many Americans, some of them unfortunately in school work, that the only "nice" people are their own kind of people; and they themselves write the definition. This attitude, however, is never snobbery pure and simple. It is perhaps one part snobbery and two parts timidity and fright. For there are a few schools which are apparently free from any impulse to discriminate; and their experience has been entirely reassuring. There is no evidence to support the apprehension that a nondiscriminatory admissions policy frightens away from private schools other desirable customers, or does damage to a school's general reputation, or militates against its usefulness. Such limited evidence as there is points in exactly the opposite direction. The misgivings of the fearful would seem to be unjustified. Yet the majority of private schools do follow an admissions policy which may not unfairly be described as a "Let's be as inclusive as we can, but let's be careful" policy.

This is a matter whose implications transcend the preferences or the prejudices of a single school. It is a question of whether the private schools mean or do not mean to put themselves, utterly and unreservedly, at the disposal of the public interest. It is not a question of whether a policy of discrimination can be legally practiced; it is a question of whether it can by any means be justified.

For things are moving, and it behooves the private schools to move with them—or, much preferably, move ahead of them—or lose their chance for real distinction, as some of them have tended at times to abdicate it in the past. The private schools are thinking about this matter now, and thinking hard. Whether they are thinking fast enough, or whether they are thinking with sufficient insight and humility and magnanimity, the outcome will reveal. My feeling is that too many of them have permitted themselves to be placed in part on the defensive.

Two things have been influential in making them start thinking. One, already treated, is the threat to their status as tax-exempt, nonprofit corporations. Some private schools have recently been adjudged taxable; others have escaped such a judgment by the skin of their teeth; still others are feeling the hot breath of prosecution only a step or two behind them. Some such schools do pay taxes, of course, and have always done so, and they are the ones which are sleep-

ing well o' nights. But after admitting that the motives of
some of the prosecutors are purely mercenary and the items
in their complaints full of ignorance and error, the situation
makes one wonder whether responsibility for the emergence
of the problem may not be laid in part to the failure of the
private school to establish itself in the public mind as an
instrument of public service rather than as a "hotbed of
privilege."

A second recent social movement which has moved the
private schools to attentive speculation is the antidiscrimi-
nation laws lately passed by several states. These laws are not
aimed exclusively at privately conducted educational institutions, but they include them. The New Jersey law, for
example, includes private schools and colleges under the
designation of places of "public accommodation"—a label
which tends to wound their sensibilities. But what the law
means is clear and plain. It means that any such institution
which rejects an applicant on grounds of race, color, creed,
or national origin will place itself in violation of the statute.
Anyone who feels himself to have been so offended may file
a complaint; and the law sets up machinery for the investigation of such complaints and vests in certain officials the
authority to make decisions. It is impossible for any respectable citizen to object to such a law as a matter of principle;
but the only educational institution that can view it with
complete equanimity is the one whose admissions policy
has repudiated the practice of discrimination, and which is
therefore plainly on the right side of the fence for all to
see. Other schools and colleges must decide whether, liter-
ally, to let the law take its course, or whether to meet the
situation head-on by taking the initiative about it. It is a
question involving considerations not only of strategy but of
statesmanship. And at the heart of it, of course, as far as the

private schools are concerned, is their dubious and uneven past record in the matter of equality of opportunity as a fundamental stipulation of American democratic education. Here, again, one feels that the private school has not got its story across; and it is impossible not to wonder whether it has clearly known exactly what story it wanted—or had—to tell.

It is necessary to say again and again that there are schools under private auspices to which these strictures do not apply at all or are relevant only in part. Yet I feel sure that to every private school teacher and administrator the problems I have referred to will have a familiar ring; that they have all given them consideration and, in some cases, the most earnest thought; and that they not only affect the general public attitude toward private schools, but are also in fact part of the real problems of the private schools themselves.

The thinking of the private school, what it tries to do, what it says about itself, how it evaluates itself, are also conditioned to some extent by enconomic considerations. In schools of inferior quality the economic motive may become engrossing: some schools will offer almost anything which can wear the color of respectability, so long as there are people who seem to want it and will pay for it. But in all schools which must depend for their existence on private patronage and benefaction—and that means all private schools —there is a temptation to defer not only to the wishes of the patrons but to their prejudices and their limitations. That is to say that in all these institutions there is a tendency toward conservatism because they do depend on private support. Schools, colleges, and universities are constantly in need of money. They must get it mainly from their graduates. They would not be human if they did not feel an impulse, however strongly and successfully they may resist it, to present their claims in such terms, and in such a framework of emotional and intellectual decorum, as not to flutter the dovecotes too roughly. I am saying merely that the temptation is always present.

It constitutes a difficult situation. One of the phenomena of American private education is that so many who have been exposed to it have never been infected by it, have never learned what it really means. These bachelors of arts or science direct their more passionate enthusiasm toward such relatively insignificant considerations as buildings, the content and yield of the institution's investment portfolio, or the percentage of victory of the football team. A graduate of a famous eastern university, calling at his Alma Mater to enter his son as a freshman, disquieted by the fact that certain of its professors entertained economic opinions which differed from his own, said good-bye to one of them with the solemn warning, "But if you teach him any new ideas, there'll be blood on the moon!" If such alumni are not only stupid but well-to-do, there is a temptation laid upon a school or college administration to tread softly in the presence of such embarrassing and benighted captiousness. The episode is admittedly extreme and unusual. The impulse toward administrative circumspection is more often pricked than bludgeoned, and there are noble examples of bold rejection of the impulse in the annals of American education. But the problem remains.

And it begets another problem—the problem of complacence. If a private secondary school has been provided with superior buildings and equipment; if it is in brisk demand and its ranks are full; if it is receiving the enthusiastic approval of its patrons and graduates, it is certainly justified in feeling pleased and grateful. But it is liable also to become

self-satisfied and uncritical: to warrant the scorn of the youth-
ful Elihu by saying of itself, "Surely we are the people."
It is liable to gauge its worth by the measure of its material
success; when, in reality, a careful reading of the General
Confession would be healthier. Or, if a school is not so blessed,
it is liable, because of normal envy, to define success as
meaning buildings and enrollment; and, when it gets them,
to rest content.

These are spiritual sins of mighty gravity. For the moment
you are convinced that your school is successful the Devil
tempts you to keep it as good as it is, rather than to make
it as good as it can be. He tries to breed in you a contentment with the average. And if he succeeds, you stop trying.
You know you can turn out a pretty slick job without too
much effort, and you settle for that. The result is that you
may just miss the quality that you are bound to serve. For
in such a process of contented lethargy it is not the middle-
of-the-road students who suffer. They are kept up to snuff.
In fact they often take up most of the time and effort of
the teachers. The ones who suffer are always the best ones.
The aim of the private school should be to train good brains
and good characters to think straight and keenly and, if
possible, fast; and also to exert themselves to the limit of
their capacities. A weakness of the private schools, widely
attested by their heads, is that few students are encouraged
or driven ever to exert themselves *to the limit*—a failing I
shall enlarge upon later. And a lot of the work that gets
done is hackwork. A lot of time and thought and energy is
spent on keeping the familiar machine running smoothly.

Today the private schools are finding it hard to lift themselves out of the sense of security they enjoyed during, say,
the fifty years ending in 1929. Since the early thirties, different
forces have come to birth and power in our American society,

forces of such dynamic drive that they are affecting the
attitudes and the destinies of all the people. It is a period of
revolutionary change, social, political, economic, egalitarian.
In it, the atmosphere in which the private school must operate
is being radically altered. It is scarcely surprising that such
schools are feeling an acute attack of nostalgia for the "good
old days." It would be a pity, however, and a serious loss to
American education, if the disease should become chronic.
The situation of such schools is felt now to be precarious.
Their impulse to try to resist the ground swell of new move-
ments and to get back to the reassuring calm of the sort of
security they had in the time that is gone could well become their own undoing.

It is all very well to be careful. It is justifiable to be conservative. But the careful and the conservative stand only
once removed from the circumspect and the cautious. What
is required of private education in America today, in colleges
and universities as well as in schools, is bold, courageous
leadership. Each such institution is called upon to clarify its
objectives and to devise procedures which may be expected
to secure them. Having done so, it must move forward with
confidence and firmness. The future is uncertain and anxious.
If we have enough assurance and endurance, it is not fearful. Let us not be timid and defeated. Believing in the value
of our purposes, we can overcome the deadening pull of
ignorance, stupidity, and intolerance.

CHAPTER V

"Easy Does It"

If the private schools are to circumvent the pitfall of complacency which is their peculiar danger, and if they are to arrive at the station to which they have been called, they must expect to face disappointment and discouragement, and they must sustain themselves by dauntless faith. For in their efforts to meet their responsibilities, they cannot operate within a self-made vacuum. The influences of the outside world will press in upon them; and particularly the influence of the values, the convictions, the prejudices, the attitudes of their patrons. All these will be woven inescapably into the pattern which the schools design, affecting its quality, its clarity, and its execution.

They are nothing new, these popular values and convictions and prejudices. They have always played upon—and plagued —our educational establishment, making its task harder. Generally speaking, the kind of schools we get, what they teach, and how well they teach it, are what the people want them to be. Our educational deficiencies, that is to say, are the deficiencies of the people and of the culture the people have wrought.

One of the things Americans like, for example, about

their educational system is that it is big, for size attracts and reassures us. Our private and public schools cost us more than $2,500,000,000 a year, and that is big business. Yet we do not require of it, or even seem to care much about, the standards of quality and performance that we demand of big business in the commercial field. There, in our development of mass production, we set ourselves the most rigorous standards in the selection of materials, in the control of the process of manufacture, and in the quality of the finished product. Yet in our manufacture of an educated citizenry we have developed no means of access to the best raw materials, no method of controlling the processes of manufacture, and no accepted standard of measuring the quality of our product. About the only things we know about American education are that a lot of people get it and that it costs a lot of money.

Parents pass on to their children their apathy toward intellectual excellence. Schoolboys demand—or, if they cannot afford it, crave and envy—the best, the last word, in radio, automobile, television. Toward yesterday's best they are scornful; toward the obsolete, derisive; with the exception, perhaps, of the jalopy, which, if sufficiently disreputable, acquires a certain raffish prestige, at which the judicious laugh. There are disreputable schools too, both public and private—educational jalopies—yet the laughter of the judicious is seldom heard. They go on and on. Since we take ourselves to be a canny, practical people, with a shrewd sense of values, it is astonishing how much money we spend year after year on wretchedly incompetent education without seeming to know or mind it. And even from our best schools we do not always demand the best or seem to want it for our children. Schoolteachers develop a chronic occupational despair listening to parents—particularly fathers

—say, "I don't care whether John and Susie are on the honor roll, and I have told them so. I shall be satisfied if they get respectable grades. I want them to be well rounded." And so often that is precisely what they turn out to be—rather like a phonograph record, and with the same singularly limited repertory. A wise old schoolmaster observed, on the other hand, that he had yet to hear a parent say, "I am not concerned that John and Susie reach their peak in health and physique. I shall be content if they merely keep out of the infirmary."

This persistent deprecation of mental superiority is the symptom and expression of a characteristic American anti-intellectualism which is the product of the way our country developed. During the early years of the Republic, when the country was limited to a fairly narrow strip of land along the Atlantic seaboard, education took root and grew, first to train men for the learned professions, which required both schools and colleges, and later for more general purposes; though patronage was in both cases limited to certain classes of society. As we began to move westward, however, and pushed on until we had finally reached the Pacific, the concerns of the people changed radically, and therefore their attitudes and their sense of values. The life of these pioneers was a hard one: "conquering the wilderness" is inconsistent with academic calm. The virtues and qualities required were specialized. These people had to have stamina, resilience, and endurance; they had to have resourcefulness and ingenuity; they had to be able to work with their hands against all sorts of grueling odds. They had to keep hold of their faith and their determination in the face of a grim reality. Now, these are all nonintellectual virtues, and they came to be characteristically American virtues. There was no time then for "book learning." A person bent on the cultivation of intellectual pursuits could not be entertained even as a luxury, let alone recognized as a useful member of society. And by the time the mighty work of expansion and settlement was completed the man of high prestige was the aggressive, energetic man, the man who "got things done," who knew how to "get ahead" in comparison with his fellows.

We are his children. We admire the qualities he admired. A large proportion of our youth receive educational training at public or private expense. Yet everyone connected with education is disturbed by the preoccupation of our people with the mediocre, the trivial, and the meretricious in recreation and amusement. The level of popular entertainment offered by radio and motion picture is far below the proper tolerance point of a nation so widely—if superficially—educated; and it belies the American credo that the more you educate the more you elevate the public taste. Mechanical amusements, the urge to be on the go—and fast—no matter where; picture magazines and the comics—but the story is familiar to every thoughtful person who is concerned with quality. And this deterioration is taking place while educational institutions are enrolling a greater and greater proportion of the population.

Among many American college graduates, men and women who have been exposed to excellence—and most typically in the American business community—the person of intellectual distinction is commonly regarded with derision or fear. When Franklin D. Roosevelt, at the beginning of his first term, summoned to his counsels a group of technical experts, some of them from academic communities, America promptly dubbed them the "Brain Trust." Some of them proved to be unfit and incompetent. But since almost all of them, when first appointed, were strangers to the American public, the derisive designation obviously could not have expressed an objective appraisal of their abilities. What it did express was the fact that, to many educated Americans, the idea of pressing into government service men who had spent their lives in concentration on some special field was absurd. People who spend their lives studying and thinking bear the stigmata of the dreamer, the impractical idealist. As long as they confine their speculations to the relative privacy of the lecture platform or the seminar the public tolerates them, as it does anything else which it regards as ineffectual but innocuous. But it does not admire them. Conservative Americans, therefore, laughed at the Brain Trust. When the New Deal legislative shoe began to pinch, the derision turned to fear. Today the expert is thought to be the "crackpot," and to call a man an "intellectual" is a reproach. Yet an intellectual is simply a person who has formed the habit of thinking and who is supposed to know a lot about something— both qualities of the educated man.

Today the fear of the unorthodox in thought and speech has reached almost panic proportions. Men and women of proved ability and indisputable integrity may at any time be subjected to public accusation and investigation at the hands of self-appointed inquisitors who make up in fervor what they lack in responsibility. "Guilt by association" is a charge requiring no proof, and it is freely made, though the innocent may suffer with the guilty. In American life today we are witnessing the beginning of a movement toward "thought control" which carries alarming implications to those of us who are concerned with the basic freedoms of the American democratic system.

Another popular force operating against the highest achievement of American schools is our growing aversion for the difficult. It is both entertaining and depressing to read through the advertising pages of popular magazines and discover how simple it appears to be to learn how to do a number of things which everyone who has tried them knows are essentially difficult. When it comes to the acquisition of cultivated accomplishments, to which many Americans are vaguely attracted by a sentimental urge toward self-improvement, the winning slogan is "Ten Easy Lessons." It is hard to resist the conviction that Americans today are doing more things more easily than any other people in recorded history. Some of them, to be sure, are not worth doing. But we keep on buying a quantity of things we don't need and can't use just because they are supposed to make something easier.

And along with this there appears to be an incalculable number of Americans who believe they can become successful, secure, and serene by reading "uplift" books as fast as they come off the presses. Schools are waging constant warfare against this juvenile—and parental—conviction that "easy does it." In this matter the public school faces a peculiar difficulty. It has been called upon during the past fifty years to minister to the needs of vastly increased numbers and of an increasing diversity of racial and national background. With the rapid growth of our urban population, also, the public school, in order to meet the capacities and the needs of its students, has had to set standards which they could meet and to expand greatly its vocational programs. This has meant serious problems, and a great deal of energy and intelligence and devotion has gone into their solution. In the process, however, standards have been lowered, and the teaching of traditional subjects such as English and arithmetic is not in fact as good as it was even ten and fifteen years ago. Today the graduates of public grade schools, by and large, do not know what they are supposed to know. Easy come, easy go.

The private school is equally the target of this social pressure to make things easy and to justify and tolerate a child's neglect of what is hard for him. "Mr. Brown and I," says a visiting mother, "always had difficulty with mathematics, and Tom unfortunately is just like us." And there sits Tom, clutching the parental dispensation gratefully to his bosom; and you are confident that, if Tom comes to your school, you can never get a decent lick of work out of him in algebra. Later you discover that, when it comes to the mastery of the batting averages of professional baseball players, Tom's scholarship is encyclopedic. "Why do you have to make your work so hard?" complains the mother of a failing student. "Peter must pass his chemistry," another writes; "I cannot have him disappointed or discouraged."

I am entirely sympathetic with the boy who faces academic failure. I have been there myself, and I know what it feels like. But the proper treatment is never parental protectiveness or oversolicitude. If failure is due to lack of effort, it should be censured by everyone concerned: the child, the parents, and the school. I am most concerned, however, with the distortion of values often observed in parental treatment of children who have done their best and still have failed. Their lot deserves sympathy, commendation, encouragement—and reclassification. It does not warrant the frequent suggestion that failure should be treated as if it were success, that accomplishment should be evaluated solely on the basis of the effort made. I am aware that conscientious effort is a major virtue, and that one cannot reasonably expect a person to do better than his best. I submit merely that the thing to do with a child who has failed in school is to find work for him which he can do and to praise him when he does it. For I cannot think of any test he will have to meet throughout his life which will not be measured by achievement rather than by effort. I can find no defense, therefore, for the practice in some public schools of promoting a child when he reaches a certain age or after he has been in the same grade for two years, regardless of whether or not he is prepared to handle more advanced work.

Nor can I justify by any means the confusion that exists in some private schools between effort and accomplishment. I do not support the worship of the great god Percentum. He has clay feet. Before a school declares that a child has failed, it should collect and consider every factor that can be adduced in his favor as a person: character, personality, citizenship, effort, future educational and vocational intentions, reputation, the possibility of unfairness in a teacher or of the fallibility of an examination. But when all is said that can be said, and still the verdict is failure, that is what it should be called. Any further effort should be expended upon repairing the damage.

The episodes I have just described reflect a combination of two common American attitudes toward education: indifference or intolerance to intellectual distinction, together with a tendency to value success in school primarily for its social implications. "Social promotion" is the term applied in the public schools to the practice of promotion and graduation on the basis of age or length of attendance rather than on the basis of accomplishment. Pressure to that end is of course implicit in the overcrowding of so many public schools; they have to let children out at the top, willy-nilly, in order to take them in at the bottom. The pressure, however, comes also from parents who fear that the retardation of their children will prove to be a reflection on them in their social relationships. As for the private schools, it has often been said that they turn out snobs. There are of course snobs among their graduates, as there are among the graduates of public schools, but I should not agree that either kind of school makes snobs. I should say, rather, that snobbish parents often crave the admission of their children into one of a group of schools which they happen to regard as socially exclusive, and calculated therefore to elevate their position in the social hierarchy. For the snob is by definition fearful and on the defensive, and it quiets the gnawing of his Philistine soul to feel that he can thank God that he is not as other men.

It is a curious irony that social compunction and solicitude should so torture the souls of a people brought up on the conviction that all men are created equal. But the condition exists and it is widespread; and by its presence or absence one can measure in part the difference between mice and men. It makes the schools' task harder.

It shows itself again, and from the same motive, in the widely held conviction that manual vocations are degrading —not personally but socially. This invidious distinction is especially prevalent in public high schools which offer college preparatory work as well as vocational training. In some such schools teachers report a tendency on the part of the college-preparatory group to feel themselves a cut above those of their fellow students who are preparing for immediate employment. In consequence, parents sometimes enroll their children in the college-preparatory group, and press for their retention in it, even though they may not be interested in it or fit for it. The effect of this snobbery is particularly damaging to the children in the vocational courses, for there is plenty of evidence to show that often they either feel themselves to be socially inferior or think that others so regard them. The situation is accentuated by the attention commonly paid to differences in economic status among the families of the students.

The effect of it is not limited to social considerations. The country has a stake in it which is far more important than that. For the kind of leadership I have been talking about must be assured for all callings and all pursuits if it is to be adequate for the country's needs. Labor in all fields of work requires the leadership of intellectually superior men and women who also, in point of character and breadth of vision, are of the highest caliber, which is precisely what the best of them have been and are. But there are too few of them, and the means for getting more are inadequate.

In a letter to the *New York Herald Tribune* in July, 1949, Joseph Belsky, Third International Vice-President, Amalgamated Meat Cutters and Butcher Workmen of North America, American Federation of Labor, points to the small number of colleges and universities that offer a fairly complete industrial relations program. "What could be done," he writes, "would be to get established universities to set up special schools of labor relations, granting their own degrees just as schools of business, accounting, engineering and pharmacy do today. Trade unions could participate financially in this venture by endowing certain specific studies, just as business firms and wealthy individuals endow 'chairs' for the study of petroleum geology or medieval French literature. . . . It might also be advisable for unions to select younger people right out of union ranks and provide scholarships for them so that they will be able to undertake such professional study."

The cause of labor and its partnership in the American enterprise must suffer irreparable damage if the attitude is permitted to prevail that people who work with their hands are for that reason inferior and contemptible and that only the white-collar class is the fit place for a free American. The private school has to fight that battle too. Its ranks include many fine persons who would be happy and useful and influential in any number of occupations commonly regarded as vocational, but whose aptitude and appetite for a liberal education are both deficient. At present these students tend to proceed with torpor and docility along the path on which their parents have set them and which they have followed for so long that they themselves have come to believe that it is the only path that will lead them anywhere. It is a sad sacrifice of varied talents and inclinations to a conventional, socially acceptable mold.

All these are influences brought to bear upon what our schools, both public and private, would like to do. Inevitably they limit the schools' achievement. They do damage to standards. They run at cross-purposes with the schools' function. Yet Americans have great faith in their schools, and their confidence in what the schools can accomplish is often touching. When the results are disappointing, the schools generally get the blame. Unfair as the reproach may be, it springs from a promising popular recognition, felt instinctively rather than rationally appraised, that the people's schools are indeed the bulwark of democracy and that, if they are effectively utilized, there is no limit to what they can do. But when the people blame the schools for failing to change society, they show also their human insistence that if society is to be changed, the change is to take place within the limits and along the lines of their preferences. In this sense, people often, though unconsciously, make the schools the scapegoats for their own deficiencies of insight and perception, for their own intransigence and narrowness. They want to eat their cake and still have it. They want to cherish the schools and still hold them at fault. And the fact that schools cannot help reflecting the limitations of their patrons makes for stalemate rather than for ordered progress.

For even if they enter at the lowest level, a school gets conditioned children. The emotional "set" is already largely determined. And the school can be only one of many forces which shape its children. Furthermore, a just evaluation of the school's influence is impeded by reason of the fact that its objectives are long-range, whereas Americans generally like to see results reached quickly. Information can be communicated fairly rapidly. It takes a long time to inculcate values. And education is concerned with values. It is an exercise in the art of communication, and communication is a highly complicated business. "Do you understand me?" someone asked Robert Louis Stevenson. "God knows," he replied; "I should think it highly improbable."

It is because it is dealing with the ultimate rather than with the immediate that education, in the opinion of an impatient public, sometimes seems to fail. Heads of private schools, at least, mourn with each other at the frequency with which they are expected to undo and do over again what has been badly—and sometimes irreparably—done before. You cannot make people over by increasing their grasp of fact. You can do it only by changing the way they feel and care; for it is what a man feels and what he cares about that determines his behavior. A man may be well informed and behave badly because he has a grasp of facts rather than a grasp of values. People do not so often fail because of ignorance as because of indifference. As Shelley says in his *Defence of Poetry*, "There is no want of knowledge respecting what is wisest and best in morals, government, and political economy. . . . We want the creative faculty to imagine that which we know; we want the generous impulse to act that which we imagine; . . . we have eaten more than we can digest." It is the task of education (and it is the only valid measure of its accomplishment) to make people better. That is why strictly vocational education must make concessions to general education for all the people; for vocational training cannot make people better: it can only make them more skillful. Any program of education, therefore, of whatever sort and at whatever level, that neglects its obligation to make people better is to that extent deficient.

That is why I dissent from those of my professional colleagues who maintain that the function of a college education is to train the mind; and particularly from college professors who say to the schools, in effect if not explicitly, "You give them the facts, and we'll teach them how to think." In the first place, you cannot train the mind alone; you cannot sharpen and refine a person's mental processes and not do anything else to him. For his mind is affected by his emotions and his imagination, by his reflexes and his digestion, by all the multitude of undiscoverable influences that have made him the person he is. The professor, therefore, who asserts that his sole concern is intellectual training is either ignorant or stupid or morally irresponsible.

Furthermore, the purpose of all training is not primarily to develop capacities, but to affect behavior. You do not train a dog to jump through a hoop in order that he may possess the competence as an abstract intellectual proposition. You do it so that, when the occasion seems appropriate, he will jump through a hoop. And when you are training not dogs but future citizens, what you are aiming at is not tricks. It is the formulation of purposes and objectives; of the individual's ability to see himself in relation to others and to the achievement of causes which are suprapersonal. It is to develop in him a sense of his meaning and destiny, and of what he can and should do about them. All this takes time. You cannot get it on short order. But because you cannot, Americans are often impatient with their schools, and expect of them what they cannot possibly deliver.

CHAPTER VI

Take Your Choice

In the exercise of their traditional right to provide for their children whatever sort of education they prefer, supporters of the private school have established one of its most striking and distinctive characteristics—its extraordinary variety. This diversity has proved to be healthy and serviceable, for it has made it possible for parents to choose among institutions which gave special emphasis to almost every aspect of education they might wish stressed. The attempt to enumerate them would be impossible and not particularly helpful, since in most cases their differences are less important than the aims they hold in common. Yet certain types of private schools are important by reason of the numbers who support them, of the nature of the aims they consider central, or of the influence they have exercised within the American school community.

Numerically the most impressive group of private schools is made up of the parochial schools under the auspices of the Roman Catholic Church. The Catholic Directory for 1949 reports, in the United States, 2,385 parochial, diocesan, and private secondary schools with an enrollment of 508,724; and 7,777 parochial grade schools with an enrollment of

2,351,604. The principles on which Roman Catholic education is based are clear and consistent. According to Monsignor Philip J. Furlong, who has been principal of New York City's Cardinal Hayes High School and secretary of education of the New York Archdiocese, "Man lives, according to Catholic teaching, to know, love and serve God. Education, which is part of living, must therefore be directed towards man's primary end." The end of education, that is to say, is a religious end. The discipline of education, therefore, is prescribed in the canon law of the church, which not only proclaims "the authority of the Church to educate" but also states plainly that "parents have a most solemn obligation to observe the law of the Church with respect to the education of their offspring." The canon law directs that "not only is nothing taught them that is opposed to the Catholic religion and good morals, but the principal place is to be held by their religious and moral education." "Young people, who attend secondary schools . . . are to be taught their religion more perfectly and more completely." But the intellectual and academic standards of Roman Catholic education are intended to be secured by the stipulation that teaching clergy are to be "outstanding" not only for zeal but for learning.

Roman Catholic education, like the religion of which it is an instrument, has as its chief purpose the salvation of souls. Pope Pius XI, therefore, in his Encyclical on the Christian Education of Youth, declares that "it is clear that there can be no true education which is not wholly directed to man's last end." "The family, therefore," he continues, "holds directly from the Creator the mission and hence the right to educate the offspring . . . a right anterior to any right whatever of civil society and of the State, and therefore inviolable on the part of any power on earth." But, the Pope adds, "It does not follow from this that the parents' right to educate their children is absolute and despotic; for it is necessarily subordinated to the last end and to natural and divine law." He finally affirms: "Accordingly in the matter of education, it is the right, or to speak more accurately, it is the duty of the State to protect in its legislation, the prior rights already described, of the family as regards the Christian education of its offspring, and consequently also to respect the supernatural rights of the Church in this same realm of Christian education."

Touching on the degree of prominence given to religious studies in Roman Catholic school curricula, the Reverend R. C. Hartnett, S.J., Editor in Chief of *America* and former Chairman of the Department of Political Science in the University of Detroit, estimates that "Religious instruction probably occupies no more than one-sixth of the time of a grade school pupil" and that "In Catholic high schools and colleges it occupies only about two hours a week." Catholic schools, he says, do not "relegate the fundamental 'tool' subjects to a place of unimportance."

Father Hartnett observes that Catholic schools have leaned "rather heavily towards a classical, or at least an academic, curriculum"; that they have been "a bit slow to allow to subjects like the social sciences what many educators—including many Catholic educators—might think is their proper place." "We have not," he writes, "established enough technical and trade schools, either, though we do have some." "Catholic educators experiment a good deal, just as do other teachers. We have our 'progressive' schools, but in general we prefer more traditional methods and insist on what we consider to be a reasonable degree of discipline."

Catholics, he says, accept it as natural that the Church should have authority in the field of education, though he declares that not all Catholics respect this authority to the full. He points to the diversity in policy among Catholic schools and dioceses, but affirms one policy which is "universal"—"that the only place for a Catholic child . . . is in a Catholic school"; a policy not only held by him but required by canon law.

Within the various Protestant communions, so-called "church schools" are not held to the enforcement of dogma and doctrine as they are under the jurisdiction of the Roman Catholic Church. Protestant church schools are usually, though by no means always, under the patronage of their churches' ruling body, whether diocese or synod or whatever, and in a few cases the church contributes to the support of its connected schools. Occasionally the statutes of a church school provide that the clergy be represented on the board of trustees, either as chairmen or as regular members. Such schools naturally practice the forms of worship used by their churches, and church doctrine is presented in the classroom.

But the religious emphasis of church schools varies widely. In some of them a systematic attempt is made to stress the religious significance of learning in all its phases. In others the academic training is secular, and religious training is provided through chapel servces and classroom instruction. The fact that the student body in Protestant schools, whether they are church connected or not, usually includes a great variety of religious affiliations undoubtedly influences the schools in determining the weight to be given to religion in their programs. Prospective patrons of private schools who are earnestly interested in the place of religion in education had best discuss the matter with heads of individual schools, for the range of practice extends from the evangelical to the indifferent, and, in extreme cases, excludes any mention or treatment of religion in the program.

Most private schools, whether day or boarding, are nonsectarian, but avowedly Christian. If they are boarding schools, they require daily chapel and Sunday church attendance, while day schools conduct services in their assembly halls. The order of service may be wholly religious in its content or consist of a mixture of the religious with matters of general school interest. The degree of ritual used is an expression of the preference of each school rather than of a strict adherence to the standard practice of a single communion. The Bible is generally taught in the classroom. The emphasis placed upon these matters in nonsectarian schools differs as widely as it does in church schools, and so does the impact and influence of the religious plan upon the lives of the students. It would be a mistake to suppose that the efficacy and vitality of religion in a school depend on whether or not it is connected with an organized church. They depend rather on what the school authorities sincerely mean them to be.

The size of a private school is a determining factor in the choice of many parents. "We have considered schools X and Y," they often say, "but we feel sure they are too big." They fear that in a large school children are left to sink or swim—the implication being that theirs would sink. They rightly want them to be treated as individuals, different from everybody else; and they are apprehensive that in a large school teachers are too busy with too many to pay real and informed attention to the needs of each, with the result that all pupils are lumped together and treated alike; that they are measured strictly by their academic accomplishment, without regard to their private problems and difficulties; and that if they fail they are more or less ruthlessly thrown aside.

Now, there can be no question that, when a school accepts a student, it takes him as he is, "with all his crimes broad blown." If the school has made a thorough study, as it should have done, of his native capacity and his previous performance, it ought to know pretty reliably what to expect of him. If it admits him under the illusion that he is better than he really is, the fault is the school's. Its subsequent treatment of him, therefore, should be tempered by a recognition of his assets and liabilities, which means that harsh and peremptory procedures cannot be justified.

Yet I have no reason to believe that a school's disregard for the individual student increases directly with its size or that there is any inherent relation between the two factors. I know of plenty of situations in which schools have been inconsiderate or insensitive or unfair in their treatment of undergraduate shortcomings, and in some of them I have been involved myself. But they have been neither limited to the larger schools nor characteristic of them. If it is felt, therefore, that in large schools size and impersonality go hand in hand, the fault lies not in the numbers but in the failure of some large schools to provide a social and academic situation in which each student is made to feel that he is cared for as an individual.

The large school can and frequently does bring to the needs of individual students all the sympathy, insight, knowledge, and concern they require and ought to have. Recruit teachers who take their guidance function seriously, provide them with full information about their charges, see to it that they are not made responsible for too many of them, and the results will be all they should be.

Some parents, on the other hand, prefer large schools for their children. Provided the units of instruction and guidance are small enough to secure the interests of each child, big school advocates find advantages in numbers. Among them the boy or girl of real distinction in any field of effort is likely to find his peers or his superiors in sufficient force to stretch his powers to the full. Whatever the merit of this contention, it is obviously subjective, since the ablest graduates of large schools are not individually more notable than those of small ones. It is held by some to be an advantage that large schools, more easily than small, can form classroom sections on the basis of native ability rather than mere grade, thus permitting the more gifted students to go further and every level of capacity to proceed at its own pace. Others, teachers and laymen both, feel that slower pupils do better work in the presence of, rather than segregated from, their brighter contemporaries.

In the general social life of a large school there is wide scope for the education of students by each other, in ways which are not less valuable because they escape the notice of the faculty. There is likely to be less scrutiny and direct control over the minute details of student life, which, though it may result in carelessness, may also cultivate a degree of self-reliance which too much admonition and correction tends to stifle. Indifference in these concerns is inexcusable. Emotional detachment, however, may be a healthy antidote to the excesses and exaggerations of parental bias.

But the various contentions about the relative merits of largeness and smallness do not cancel out and leave an objectively valid conclusion. They cannot be reduced to a formula whose terms may be expected to yield the "right answer." The soundest procedure for parents, subjective and impressionistic as it is, is to visit several types of schools, all of them known to be of good quality, and choose the one whose personalities and general atmosphere give them the most comfortable and reassuring feeling.

The population of private day schools is much larger than that of boarding schools. It is probable that some parents choose day rather than boarding schools for their children because they cost less. The outstanding argument offered in behalf of the day school, however, is that it presents a sound education under high standards without breaking the ties of family life, and this is so because the assurance of family solidarity, of membership in a closely knit group, is of basic and irreplaceable importance to a child's emotional security. A school enjoys a great advantage if it can attack the problems of a child's development in co-operation with its parents, if it can treat him at the same time as a member of a school and of a family too. The organization of parent-teacher groups also, if programs are intelligently planned and meetings kept to the point, may develop a community of understanding as well as interest which can be of the greatest benefit. It is possible for day schools to educate parents along with their children—a need on the whole neglected in America—and thereby to affect their attitudes toward education and their sense of values. There are instances of important alterations in community standards and practices accomplished through the initiative of day schools. The fact, too, that children are going to school in the same neighborhood in which they live gives to the motivation provided by the school a ready outlet for expression on the civic level. Children are surrounded by the typical problems of an American community, whose proximity, if properly exploited, enlightens their awareness of the interrelationship between education and adult responsibility.

The boarding school, of course, is its own community, artificial in the sense that its students are nonresident and therefore have no stake in the towns and villages in which most such schools prefer to establish themselves. The disadvantages of this situation are implied in what has just been said of day schools. Yet the American boarding school has a continuous history which reaches back two hundred years at least, and nobody would deny that it is a permanent and characteristic feature of our educational landscape.

Perhaps its greatest asset as an instrument of education is that its whole life is under control. Every hour of the twenty-four is part of a general plan of activity and leisure; the relevance of each aspect of school life to all the others is predetermined rather than accidental. The influence of the day school on its students extends of course far beyond the substance of its daily program; but its control over their activities stops when the school day is over. Then they are subject to all the competitive distractions that a typical residential environment contains: movies, radio, television, parties; and most particularly the consequences of the fact that parents are not uniformly firm or consistent in enforcing the school's expectations in regard to evening activity, the strictness of some being unfavorably compared by their children with the leniency of others. The necessity of eliminating distractions which cannot be controlled without constant struggle is an important reason why some parents send their children to boarding schools.

Despite great differences in physical equipment, life at most boarding schools is on the whole simple. More important, it is the same for everyone. People of modest or slight means sometimes hesitate to patronize boarding schools for fear their children, associating with those who come from families of larger income, will feel embarrassed or humiliated or become discontented or disgruntled. Nothing is less likely to happen. At a boarding school everybody gets what everybody else gets and no more. The regime provides no opportunities for ostentation by the well-to-do. Nothing within it calls attention to differences in economic status. A visitor who followed the school program through a single day would find no reliable means of distinguishing between rich and poor. Such considerations as money, dress, automobiles, social standing, financial position, which plague the day school, whether it is public or private, have little if any influence in a boarding community.

It cannot, of course, provide the intimacies of home and family life. But in a time when home standards are widely in decline and the stability of the family is in increasing jeopardy, one cannot escape the rueful conclusion that some children are better off away from their parents. And as for the happily great majority who come from sound homes, the boarding schools offer them a supplemental benefit which is acknowledged by parents in large numbers. During the years when a child is proceeding through the main phases of his emotional development, making the crucial adjustments to himself, his parents, his brothers and sisters, he needs to be a member of a family, and his separation from it, for whatever reason, is likely to produce serious consequences later. Once his security is won, however, there is plenty of evidence that he matures faster away from home in many cases. At a boarding school he is treated carefully, but without the emotional preoccupation that it is difficult for parents to transcend, and which, if it is overpossessive or overprotective, may retard the development of self-reliance. Parents repeatedly express incredulous surprise at the degree to which their children have matured at the end of so short a period as a single term at a boarding school. The reason seems to be that, at a school away from home, the girl or boy belongs to an independent and separate community, no longer to a family group in which the parents are necessarily the dominant members; in which the prohibitions and incentives, applying to all alike, are free of the emotional implications surrounding parental admonitions.

Given a united family and good schooling at home, a

boarding school, if it is given consideration at all, can be most useful when a child seems clearly ready and eager to try his wings by himself. The symptoms occur at different ages. Frequently they appear as a child gradually discovers that his parents are much older than he used to think they were and that their ignorance of life is appalling; and when his naturally forgiving nature cannot contain its bounds and sours into captiousness and fault-finding. At that period separation sometimes does wonders.

Day and boarding schools offer the same thing in point of academic training. Their important differences express different but not necessarily contradictory opinions about the best environment for child development up to the point of entrance into college or the discontinuance of formal schooling. Each type has its devoted advocates, and again, as in the comparison between large and small schools, there is no conclusive argument for one as against the other. Their occupancy of the same area is valuable chiefly in broadening the limits of choice open to prospective patrons.

One of the most interesting and important options offered to the patrons of private schools is the choice between segregation and coeducation. Public secondary education has traditionally been coeducational since Horace Mann instituted such schools in Massachusetts in 1826, though some educational historians believe the reason was financial economy rather than the exemplification of a theory, and though a few public secondary schools, chiefly in the East, practice the segregation of the sexes. Before 1900, on the other hand, private secondary schools in the United States served primarily either boys or girls separately, and even in the private elementary schools nearly half the pupils were so segregated. Today segregation is still the rule in nearly half the country's private secondary schools; though with the beginning of the country day school movement after the turn of the century, which was planned to combine the best features of the boarding and the day school, these new schools usually became coeducational.

The number of private coeducational boarding schools is very small indeed. Those who administer them—and they are likely to be Friends schools—hold the view, with considerable logic and reason, that theirs alone are truly coeducational institutions; that mixed day schools, both public and private, merely teach boys and girls together in the same classroom and segregate them for everything else—a practice which amounts to coinstruction rather than full coeducation.

The opinions of the average person on these matters are usually the product of preference, prejudice, or custom. They cannot well be anything else, for there is a surprising scarcity of scientific studies on the subject. Psychology and psychiatry have had little to say about it. That there is a conflict of viewpoint among laymen is evident, but the reasons for it are conjectural rather than factual.

The belief persists in some educational quarters that since boys and girls develop at different rates during adolescence they present different kinds of learning needs which can be better met if they are educated separately. What the psychiatrist would have to say about this would depend, I suspect, on his own professional experience. Heads of boys' schools would be likely to agree, I think, that certain incentives and methods owe their effectiveness in part to the fact that the community is all male, that the atmosphere of school life derives a portion of its strength from its masculinity, which makes relatively easy the realization of the constructive implications of hero worship. Whether the father-son relationship, important to recognize in the common life of boys and men teachers, could better be rationalized under coeducation is a question to which there is so far no scientific answer.

Some parents believe that, since the problem of controlling children has grown more difficult under the complexities of modern living and broader concepts of freedom, coeducation is likely to distract children from serious concentration on formal education. Another familiar motive for the segregation of boys is the misgiving of some parents at the predominance of women teachers in the public schools, which they consider an increasing problem as boys grow older.

Certainly segregation is common in private education in America by reason of the mere force of tradition. When the earliest of our private schools were founded, segregation was the practice in England and Europe, which provided us with models, and as later schools were inaugurated they followed the familiar convention. To extreme experimentalists in education, all tradition is likely to be thought of as a moss-grown survival, productive only of snobbery and complacency. The "old school tie" has a bad name among such radical observers. Yet respect for tradition may be a conserver of values real and permanently valid, not merely sentimental and reactionary; and disrespect, by the same token, may indicate callous perceptions rather than acute insight. Tradition, to be sure, may represent inertia. It may also be the guiding force toward high action and noble ends. A people has a way of doing things which is its own, however impossible it may be to justify it rationally. As long as segregation in our private education offers values which seem to its patrons genuine and important, it will not only of course continue to be practiced; it will continue to contribute to the national life. The social prestige of a segregated school is an ignoble measure of its value. An ideal of service is a permanent good and a worthy criterion.

Yet the proponents of coeducation suggest that a school for boys and a school for girls are, as Burton S. Fowler, headmaster of Germantown Friends School, puts it for them, "only half-worlds. The warped environment thus provided in individual cases and even for society as a whole may have ominous consequences, which are all the more serious because they are covered up." The argument lends new weight to the observation that the question of coeducation is answered more frequently by speculation than by scientific analysis. For the disinterested observer would scarcely draw the conclusion that separately educated men and women act like products of a "warped environment," or that their behavior as citizens and parents is fraught with implications which, all the more because they are concealed, may issue in "ominous" consequences for themselves and for society as a whole.

The argument for coeducation is that, since we live in a society which is bisexual physically and, in increasing degree, sociologically, it is logical and natural that boys and girls, at all ages, should work, play, study, and grow up together, and thus achieve mutual respect and understanding. The very fact that in all the relationships of life boys and girls make different as well as similar contributions suggests that each sex is essential to the other. Segregation overlooks the fact that, in both emotional and intellectual characteristics, the variations within each sex are often quite as great as those between the sexes. Finally, it is held, there is doubtful wholesomeness in separating boys and girls at the very age when a sound adjustment to each other is the most vital biological and social need of their lives. The coeducational school is a laboratory for the study and practice of human relationships.

Here the argument rests, in the absence of data to resolve it. It cannot be demonstrated that boys and girls who have been educated separately have displayed social and civic qualities which mark them as better adjusted to the demands of American life than the products of mixed schools. Neither can the opposite contention be demonstrated. There is no conclusive evidence in support of the conviction that separately educated men and women face peculiar difficulties in the achievement of happy marriage and successful domestic life. It is hardly possible for a parent or a teacher to justify his convictions or to say anything about them except that he happens to hold them. The important consideration is that a decision be reached on what seem to be the merits of the question, without prejudice and beyond the constraints of custom or expediency.

PART TWO

The Program of the Private School

CHAPTER VII

What To Teach and How To Teach It

If it is the special role of the private school to cultivate excellence, it is under heavy obligation when it goes about the establishment of its course of study. Formal education is an exercise in the difficult art of communication. The decision of what shall be communicated is momentous and far-reaching. And it is at this point that schools are especially liable to embrace apostasy and follow false gods; for the question of what our schools should teach has been argued with heat and violence for the past twenty-five years.

It ought to be possible to say, without fear of rebuttal, that a course of study aimed at the cultivation of excellence should be limited to material selected because of its inherent distinction, its established merit. No sooner is this said, however, than critical questions are raised—and honest questions too, for which reasonable and persuasive answers must be found. Who is to judge which material is inherently distinguished, which has established merit? How can we be sure that what has been taught for centuries really has shaping and creative power under radically different and rapidly shifting social circumstances? Is it not offered now simply because it always has been offered, and because it is easier to continue

with it than to face its inadequacies and adopt material more
relevant to modern world conditions and therefore more
likely to encourage excellence as it should be defined today—
namely, as the fulfillment of the needs and wishes of the
people as they see them? Is not the perpetuation of the pat-
terns of the past nothing more or less than a conspicuous
example of cultural lag?

These questions clearly express a mighty skepticism, in the
minds of those who ask them, about the answer to an anterior
question which they rightly feel to be of great importance:
Can there be any permanently valid standards, perdurable
and above the vicissitudes of change?

The answer of the private school must be an unequivocal
Yes, and it is the one voice that can make it.

It is perennially interesting to ask secondary school students this question: Is the Mona Lisa great painting, a sym-
phony of Brahms great music, inherently and undeniably and
beyond opinion; or are they great only as you happen to
think so; and would boogie-woogie and the comics be just
as great if most people thought they were? Answers are always divided; and their divergencies are at the heart of the
controversy over what should be studied in our schools.
Those who believe that greatness is inherent do not suppose, of course, that any definition of it can be absolute, any
gauge of it totally objective. They see that greatness is relative, comparative. But they do accept the existence of a
scale of values: they are sure that some music, for example,
seems to them cheap and trivial in comparison with other.
They confess that their failure to appreciate reputedly great
music may signify the poverty of their own critical perceptions rather than an intrinsic absence of merit in the work
itself; and they concede that the opinion, in any field of
art, of people who live and work in it, who know its prob-

lems and how well or ill they are met, who are also apparently most sensitive to its significance, are best qualified to express judgments which the layman may accept as valid. Their brethren of the "I don't know anything about art, but I know what I like" school have much to answer for in the debauching of popular standards; and their elders of the same critical indolence and passivity would turn schools into educational bargain counters in which cut-rate sales were available every day.

To any reasonably mature intelligence it is obvious that the quality of a man's mind is determined by the kind of material to which he directs it. Furthermore, the quality of his mind, the sort of mental exercise to which he has put it, establishes his adequacy in all the relationships of his life— civic, economic, political, and domestic. If he confines his reading to trash, he will be a trivial person. If he limits his mind to the consideration of material whose relevance is immediate utility, he will grow more skillful but no wiser. The private school, therefore, must let no consideration of expediency, no popular advocacy of fads or specious formulas, to unsettle its faith that a perception of what is good and true and beautiful can be derived only from a plan of study which contains the best that has been thought and said.

Some historians of American education have observed that our earliest schools taught the classics because they were accustomed to them and because they were required training for the ministry and other learned professions which it was the schools' chief function to supply. Such schools, they point out, offered vocational training to a selected few; and when their function had grown obsolete, they vanished. The observation is factually true. Yet it is absurd to say that the classical curriculum, with all its narrowness, had no

educational significance except as a quaint and archaic survival of a priestly tradition; and it is altogether misleading
to refer to it as vocational in the same sense as the word
is used today.

The old curriculum had in view not merely the acquisition of a prescribed body of knowledge. It was also and
much more importantly intended to establish in those who
pursued it certain qualities of mind and spirit which were
held to be of general worth. It aimed at elevation and enlightenment as well as information. It was supported by a concern for the dignity and the destiny of the individual as
well as for his workaday accomplishments. It is possible to
argue that it was not the curriculum best calculated to
achieve its own ends, though such a hypothesis would be
difficult to sustain, and it is perfectly evident that it was
too rigid and too limited to set the pattern for the education
of the American people. But the object of education, today
as always, is, in the phrase of the late Stuart P. Sherman,
"Shaping Men and Women." Its end is a moral end. Democracy is an ideal, not merely a succession of activities. Unless education continues to be devoted to making men better,
as well as to developing their techniques, it cannot advance
the democratic cause that it is designed to serve.

The men who laid the foundations of this country were
interested in ideas; they were devoted to ideals. They espoused them when it was dangerous to do so. They were
given strength to do so by faith. They were possessed by the
conviction that every individual had rights which it was
their firm purpose to secure. In other words, they had fixed
standards and values. These revolutionary zealots were by no
means always intellectuals. The movement they fostered gave
expression to plenty of rabble-rousing and demagoguery. It
was intemperate as well as passionate. The most gifted among

them did, to be sure, produce documents in the field of political theory and practice which have scarcely been approached in power of thought and depth of insight. But factionalism and bitter conflict of conviction were so intense as to threaten the very survival of the new national enterprise. It was a saving grace that the intellectual leaders of the time were men whose political philosophy was rooted in what men had thought and said before them; that their sense of present need was shaped and guided by their knowledge of the past; that their choices expressed a belief in the existence of points of reference which were reliable for all men at all times. That the principles of eighteenth-century rationalism, which pervaded much of their thinking, have lost their promise and their dominance is not important for modern American education. It ought to take earnestly to heart, however, the continuity, the progressive development of thought which ties the present to the past, for without such a recognition of the value of historical perspective it is launched upon the open sea without a compass.

Believing these things, the private school has stood for the unchanging validity of certain values and standards. It has opposed the materialistic philosophy that everything is after all a matter of opinion and that therefore one man's opinion is just about as good as anybody else's. The problems of man, his real needs, it affirms, may not be regarded as the casual phenomena of a particular here and now. They are permanent, timeless; the same yesterday, today, and forever. To ignore what the greatest men in the past have had to say about them is not only impoverishing but absurd. This theory of the proper content of education holds also that moral values are absolute, though moral codes may differ about their relative importance; that there *is* a truth about the universe and man's place in it. Man's recognition of a measure of truth or justice in other men affirms his concept of an ideal truth and an ideal justice; and the record of the past gives him faith that he can move toward his ideal, and sheds a light upon his way.

The sort of education the private school has traditionally offered is the sort that makes men free. Through the centuries it has been called a liberal education: an education that liberates people, that frees them from ignorance, bigotry, and prejudice. It trains their recognition of what things are of most worth by giving them a scale of values to live by. It sharpens people's mental powers. It refines and makes sensitive their emotions and their imaginations. It aims to put them in full possession of their faculties and to move them to place their faculties at the service of their fellow men. The liberal education does not train people in any particular way of making a living. It tries to train them in a way of living. And if the private school is also a Christian school, it believes that truth does make men free—free to serve the will of God, however they may see it, with devotion and consecration.

The content of the liberal arts curriculum today is of course immeasurably broader than would have been considered either necessary or desirable three hundred years ago. The classics, to be sure, held their central place much longer than their alleged sterility as vehicles of culture would have led one to suppose. Gradually the "Latin requirement" in schools and by colleges yielded before the pressure of new syntheses of subjects; but it is only in recent years that colleges and universities have dropped it altogether, and it is still a "must" in a few secondary institutions. Greek as an optional subject is now caviar to the general, and there are many who regard its decline as an impoverishment of the curriculum rather than merely as a regrettable waning of an old tradition. The expanding importance of technology in American society has won a greater place for science and mathematics, and the importance of a knowledge of history to the understanding of contemporary problems has increased the time devoted to its study. Schools today offer opportunities in music and art, both in theory and in practice. The typical private school curriculum, in short, has become so rich and so diversified that it is hard to see how anyone can speak of it as narrow or rigid or out of date.

As to its practical utility in a highly mechanized setting, technical institutions are asserting increasingly their conviction that the preparatory training of prospective engineers should stress the humanistic subjects. And Dr. Willard Cole Rappleye, Dean of Columbia University's Faculty of Medicine, believes that "So-called 'premedical' education should be abolished in the colleges . . . There is no such thing as 'premedical' education, nor should students in colleges who plan to enter professional schools be regarded as premedical or predental students. [College] education is not 'pre' anything, but should be devoted to the objective of providing as broad a cultural education as the institution can provide. It should be a preparation not for medicine or dentistry or public health, but for life." And in the general opinion there is evidence of apprehension that our technological skills have outstripped our capacity to understand their implications and our concern for their use. There is a swing back to the humanities, back to a sense of the importance of values, born of a growing awareness that without vision the people perish. There is reason to believe that liberal education today is faced with the opportunity to make a uniquely valuable contribution to the country's welfare.

The liberal curriculum is peoccupied with ideas rather than with facts. It insists upon the mastery of facts, for it is impossible for anyone to know the value of what he does

not understand, and a great deal of fuzzy thinking is circulated by people who have strong convictions which, without
the data to support them, are really prejudices. But it knows
that facts alone lack power or meaning. Ideas are generalizations drawn from facts; they are interpretations of facts; they
may become the force through which facts are put to use
in the affairs of men. A man in possession of an idea may be
as infertile as a hen sitting on a china egg. An idea in possession of a man becomes kinetic and at times explosive. A liberal
education aims to teach not only the facts, but the ability to
evaluate the facts, to draw logical conclusions from them; and
finally to inspire men to the support and the advancement of
the ideas they hold to be important. This training engages
not only the mind, but the will and the spirit. It brings to
bear upon human life all the resources of personality. It
affirms the sterility of knowing that does not issue into doing.
Its ultimate intention is to affect behavior and to do so
qualitatively rather than quantitatively.

In response to critics who charged him with confining
himself to the harshly fatalistic aspects of human affairs,
Thomas Hardy asserted that a literary artist becomes vocal
in reaction only to certain special facets of life and not to
all of them. In the same fashion, students of the liberal curriculum do not respond equally to all the branches of learning
that it compasses. One of its aims at the secondary level,
therefore, should be to present to everyone the rudiments of
the chief ways in which great men have thought about man
and his world; the main efforts they have made to find the
truth about the form and meaning of the universe and of
man's place in it. In this respect it becomes an orientation
course in the humanities, with the end in view that a student,
acquainted with the elements of the various fields of human
thought, may choose for full exploration those to which he

finds himself most naturally responsive, most instinctively drawn. The child who is invited to choose which subjects he would like to look at and which ignore is being asked to make a crucial decision quite beyond his powers. To make him free also to drop a subject as soon as it fails to engage his interest is to leave him forever the prey of whim and fancy. He must be given a glimpse of the whole panorama of human thought and then allowed to choose the part of it on which he wants to concentrate.

He learns about mathematics and science, therefore, not because of their value as mental disciplines—which they also are—but because they record man's restless search for ways of measuring the universe and discovering how it is composed. He reads history not to learn facts—which it is well for him to know—but because history is the annals of what men have done as social, political, and economic creatures and an interpretation of the reasons why they have done it— the sort of hindsight that is the prerequisite of intelligent foresight, without which the present is fearful, confusing, and inscrutable. The study of the language and the literature of foreign countries gives insight into other cultures, and understanding of other ways and modes of thought—an antidote to chauvinism and provincialism. Finally, a knowledge of one's own language and literature makes one privy to the aspirations and the hopes, the tragedy and the failure, the depths of meanness and the heights of nobility, which are contained within the human heart and of which inspired men have spoken.

This is neither old nor modern; it is timeless. It is not narrow and removed from life; it is as broad as humanity and it *is* life; or else we had better have a universal burning of the books and start all over again.

Those who indict the private school most vociferously as

being archaic and "stuck fast in yesterday" have in common the fixed idea that its teaching material and methods are formal, rigid, and sterile. Will the "new" curriculum find use for the "older" subjects? asks one of them. The answer is Yes, which is reassuring. "For instance, formal grammar will be tested on the basis of what it means to the better expression of these youth, both oral and written; it will not be retained on the grounds of so-called disciplinary values." That, I take it, in addition to being poor "expression," is a good example of flogging a dead horse. I know of no good private school which gauges the value of formal grammar by any other measure or would seriously consider presenting it merely as an exercise in mental discipline. It is the sort of condescending, contemptuous misrepresentation that becomes tiresome and a little irritating because it exhibits an ignorance which could so easily be corrected if the critic wished. And it is characteristic of its kind in its implied disparagement of "disciplinary values," for which this critic has a low regard.

What do the prophets of progress offer us to replace the outworn shibboleths of the past? They urge upon us "life adjustment education," courses in "family living," "education for life," "correlation and integration," "atomic age education," "education for creative living." The advocates of these vague, general, and splendid slogans sound like gentlemen of nervous disposition and insufficient occupation who want to change the methods and the purposes of education overnight to solve a particular problem which has frightened them. Such agitated people seem to feel that nothing is permanently good; that no truths are always true; that no values are always sound. They seem not to realize that the problems of the world are old, not new, and that they are to be solved not by what people know but by what sort of people they are.

Book learning, they say, is derivative, secondhand, ivory-towerish. "We learn," they say, "what we live." "Learning by doing" is the thing. But everything we live is not worth learning. And everybody knows that we can and do *apply* what we learn to what we do. The general attitude of the critics would logically lead them to declare that an incident that occurred almost two thousand years ago and is recorded in a single ancient book could be of no relevance to modern man. Yet the influence of Jesus in the lives of men has been the most important fact of human history. The ideas of Plato can and do shape the way men feel and the way they behave, though he and Socrates would not receive a place in the "new" curriculum. And the music of Bach raises men to heights they could not scale by any amount of "doing."

The opinion that the curriculum of the private school is a fossil survival and that its teaching methods are stiff and desiccated is not corroborated by anything I know. In the best private schools the teaching is often brilliant, imaginative, resourceful, and stimulating. When its critics call its material old-fashioned and irrelevant, they are implying that to a vigorous, modern boy or girl it must be also dull. That is not true. Shakespeare and the English poets, Euclid, the literature of European cultures, the resources of history and science are not dull. The record of the creative achievements of the richest minds cannot be dull. They are felt to be so by dull people, or made to seem so by dull teachers. And it must be admitted that they are not everybody's meat. But for those who are up to them, they are the most nourishing meat. The ablest boys and girls, in both the public and the private schools, take to them. The careful study of great material is always exciting and rewarding to young people of distinct capacity, and the stricter and more exacting it is the better they like it. Good minds are formed by meeting and overcoming difficulties, by being stretched and strained.

They are formed, that is to say, by discipline. The cultivation and enrichment and strengthening of the best minds are not the only objectives of democratic education, but they are important ones. The private school curriculum is intended to attain them.

Now, to offer the best materials for education—the best "book learning"—under the highest standards is not good because it is difficult; it is difficult because it is good. It calls, in those who pursue it, for moral fiber, strength of mind, and constancy of purpose. It calls for faith too, for its objectives are remote and long-range.

For these reasons the private school is under pressure all the time to dilute it, to make it more pleasant and palatable, easier to digest and absorb; or, even more damagingly, to aim it at more proximate and more utilitarian ends. The study of the Spanish language and literature, for example, is a sound educational pursuit. Of late years its patronage has increased rapidly. Yet there can be no doubt in the mind of a schoolteacher that the choice of Spanish is often made by students who feel that it is easier than French or German; that it may be useful in business; and that Greek and Latin are idle preoccupations for a sensible person because they are dead languages. Some regard chemistry as easier than physics, and so choose it; while enrollment in biology is not limited to those who have a consuming interest in genes and hormones.

My classical colleagues tell me it is almost impossible to find a beginner's Latin book with any bite or substance; that most "modern" texts are sugar coated and diluted so as to taste good and go down painlessly; and the effort of swallowing is negligible because there is so little to swallow.

In discussing the importance of maintaining high standards, I am far from advocating their glorification. They must not be permitted to become an academic guillotine, with the faculty a group of pedagogical Madame Defarges counting the heads with grim satisfaction as they fall. When a student is accepted, not only he but the school assumes an obligation, which the school cannot pretend to discharge by dismissing him summarily for failure to meet the standards. I have in mind the general and pervading impulse, emphasized before, toward mediocrity.

It shows itself in another aspect in the emphasis placed on "interest" and "usefulness" by many students and their parents. Teachers are frequently told, when "required" subjects are under discussion, that you cannot expect a pupil to do his best work in a subject that does not interest him. A proper response would be to ask at what point the interest is deficient, whether in the pupil or in the subject. I am inclined to echo the Chestertonian aphorism that there is no uninteresting work; there are only uninterested workers. The late President Lowell of Harvard said that there is no more evidence to support the thesis that work springs from interest than the opposite thesis that interest springs from work. It was his view that a person who gives close and persistent study to a subject of intrinsic merit and importance generally ends by becoming interested in it. And over and over again the first impression of lack of interest comes from a lack of understanding of what the objectionable subject really is.

Furthermore, whether something is interesting or not may depend on circumstances. I am myself uninterested in gardening and repelled by its tools. Give me a shovel and bid me dig a garden bed, and I will tell you that digging does not interest me. But if my friend were buried under a landslide, and I had a shovel, digging would be the one thing

under the sun that would interest me—at least until I had
got him out.

The common complaint that Latin and mathematics and
chemistry are not "useful"—"because I'm going into my
father's business and won't need them"—is similarly subject
to the vagaries of circumstance. When my car is in a service
station and my tank full, a gallon of gasoline, to be sure,
is not useful to me. At the end of a day's run, with my
tank empty and fifty miles from the nearest pump, I would
pay through the nose for it. In neither case should I be justified in making a general observation about the usefulness
of gasoline.

The analogy is limited; it does not dispose of the argument; it merely exhibits one of its weaknesses. Its real
threat to standards becomes clear when one hears not school
children but professional curriculum makers talking about
"useless knowledge" and subjects which have no "practical
utility," or taking with apparent seriousness the position
that, for the training of the mind, one subject matter is as
effective as another; that bookkeeping and shopwork may
be made as potent in the shaping of mental keenness as mathematics or science. This is to suggest that, in the cultivation
of musical taste, MacDowell's *Woodland Sketches* contain
as much inherent richness as Bach's *Mass in B Minor*; or
that, when it comes to poetry, a choice between Edgar Guest
and John Keats is a toss-up. The plain fact is that, in any
training touching the mind, the imagination, and the emotions, some materials are intrinsically superior to others. To
believe otherwise is to lower standards.

In much of the current literature of curriculum making I
find repeatedly the assertion that advocates of the "traditional"
curriculum regard it as an end in itself instead of a means to
an end, which is not true; that it is generally taught in a dog-

matic, uncritical, take-it-or-leave-it, routine way, which is not true; and that it has no significance unless the values and ideals that it inculcates are brought to bear, by its students, on the problems of contemporary life, which is of course entirely true. I have already remarked that it is not the best course of study for all the people, but only for that proportion of our school population who have the capacities that its pursuit requires. The problems of democracy were not born yesterday. Neither are they peculiarly American problems. They are the age-old problems that men have always faced in their attempt to live with themselves, their fellows, and their God. They are recorded in literature with the wisdom, the joy, the indignation, and the magnanimity of genius. They are contained in the record of history. They are expressed in man's endless and inspired search for the truth about the physical universe, and through the fruitful meditations of philosophers and mystics. The artists have seen visions which uplift the eyes of earthbound, weary mortals. Surely to read the record is an enlargement of the soul.

Shakespeare or "life adjustment education"? "Atomic age education" or the history of modern Europe? The Bible or a course in "family living"? Which lead more surely to "creative living"?

Well, if you ask enough people, you get some discouraging answers.

A few years ago *Fortune* conducted a survey, directed by Elmo Roper, in collaboration with a Committee on Post-War Planning at Yale. A cross section of the entire adult population was canvassed by personal interviews, and a questionnaire was sent by mail to a cross section of college graduates.

One of the survey questions asked people to say what things they thought it was most important for their sons to get out of college. More than half replied that vocational training was the *most* important function of colleges, and 86.6 per cent said it was *very* important. Of course there is a sense in which all education is vocational. A great many young people go into it during or after high school. Others proceed to professional training after college. It ought not to be surprising, therefore, that the poll revealed a sense of the preponderant importance of vocational training. The significant thing, as Frank D. Ashburn has pointed out, "is rather in the overwhelming sense of the public that such training should take place in the undergraduate years, which for as long as our idea of a college has existed have been held as the sacred precincts of a liberal education."

Second place in the "most important" rating was occupied by "ability to get along with and understand people"; and under the heading of "very important" it got a higher percentage of votes than anything else. Of those questioned, 17.7 per cent thought the most important acquisition was "desire and ability to be a more useful citizen"; 13.8 per cent believed it was "ability to think more logically"; only 10 per cent gave supremacy to "moral growth," though 74.8 per cent believed it was very important. The accumulation of facts rated low as a collegiate value, and less than half of those polled considered appreciation of literature and the arts important.

It is risky business, of course, to draw conclusions from replies to a questionnaire: there is a tendency to find in it what you want to find. In studying the results of this one, however, it seems clear that the palm goes to "useful" and "practical" accomplishments and last place to the "cultural" values—those having to do with the enlargement of individual capacities and perceptions—though most of the people had a good word to say for them.

Now, knowing how to earn a living is obviously essential

for everybody, though it is doubtful that a college is the best place to learn it, because the college will distract a man's attention to a number of other matters which are of no economic value; and I should say that four years is longer than you need. The advocates of the liberal tradition, furthermore, agree with the American public that it is important for everybody to be able to understand other people and get along with them, so long, at least, as there is no implication of the purpose to get *ahead* with them or through them: the "young man on the make" sort of thing. Liberal education has always placed importance on this matter. But I suspect that even these adherents of the utilitarian would confess that what distinguishes one person from another is the strength of his character, the breadth and scope of his mind, his tolerance and sympathy, and other qualities which have nothing to do with vocational skill or amiability. It is that sort of person liberal education is intended to develop. The private secondary school is devoted to that end. The scale of values reflected by the *Fortune* poll is immature at best and at its worst is disturbing. But it represents a movement and a trend, and all who are interested in our schools must attend to it. For if we throw overboard the liberal tradition, the loss would be tragic.

The private school's purpose to stimulate potential excellence to the top of its bent is impeded by certain characteristics of American practice and incentive within the schools themselves. An experienced English observer has remarked, for example, that in this country "few boys are encouraged or driven ever to exert themselves *to the limit*." An American teacher with experience in England asserts that "In comparison with the scope and maturity of the projects undertaken" by the top scholars at a good English public school, much of the work of outstanding scholars in a comparable American private school "is immature and elementary, however time-consuming." It is the friendly English critic's opinion that the cult of "getting by," which attracts to its membership untold thousands of mediocre Americans, includes also too many of the ablest students, who are content to do work which, in comparison with that of the majority, is only relatively superior when it might be really distinguished. In the best English schools the academic leaders have great prestige and exercise significant intellectual leadership. In America the familiar investiture in office of the athlete or the boy of attractive personality tends to perpetuate a sort of leadership which, though often wholesome and morally commendable, does not affect the intellectual tone of the school.

Of the several factors that have brought about the situation in America, perhaps the most important is the fact that in our private boys' secondary schools almost everybody wants to go to college, which is far from being the case in England. There the university scholarship examinations, success in which carries honor and prestige, are of a rigor beyond the knowledge of Americans, and even the Higher Certificate Examinations, written by English candidates for university admission, though less difficult than the scholarship examinations, are searching and exhaustive in their demands. The degree of difficulty of our College Board examinations, on the other hand, is slightly less than that of the preliminary School Certificate examinations that English boys take two or three years before they leave school. Our best boys, that is to say, for purposes of admission to college, must meet a standard so easily within their grasp that it offers little if any incentive to supreme exertion. Whatever pressure they are under must be provided by their schools, whose charge, as Arthur Perry, headmaster of Milton Academy, puts it, is the development of those powers which will enable a boy "to think his way through college rather than remember his way into it." But it is a pity that the job can be done both ways.

The present situation leads some critics of the private school to the conclusion that, academically speaking, it is under the thumb of the colleges, that its course of study is arbitrarily imposed upon it by college requirements, and that these requirements are what they are because professors have a vested interest in their own subjects and intend to keep it.

Now, there is no doubt that many private school pupils ought not to go to college; they have neither the appetite nor the capacity for higher education, and they seek it only for reasons of social and business preferment. They ought to give up formal education after they have completed the secondary level.

But it does not follow at all that a course of study which meets the requirements for college admission is inappropriate for those who do not go to college; and it is a contradiction of the facts to say that the private secondary school curriculum is what it is because the colleges insist upon it. The colleges insist upon evidence of superior capacity and performance; and in my experience, when a departure from the stated entrance requirements seems to a school to be in the best interests of a student, the college permits it.

Yet the influence of college entrance examinations and admission requirements on the private secondary schools cannot be summarily dismissed. An inquiry directed to a considerable number of such schools revealed wide variations in the degree to which their teaching methods, their own internal examinations, and their grading standards reflected their concern for a creditable performance by their pupils in the examinations of the College Entrance Examination Board. Now, it is clearly the province of colleges and universities to set their own entrance requirements, whether the candidates and the schools that prepare them happen to like them or not. And it is the plain duty of the preparatory schools to fit their students for college admission if their abilities are adequate. In performing this duty the schools would be derelict indeed if they failed to maintain standards at least as high as those of the institutions in which their pupils intended to enroll. But the evidence is impressive that too many private schools direct their classroom procedures, deliberately and unduly, toward preparing their students for the College Boards; and that many teachers, and therefore inescapably their pupils, are too conscious of the Boards and too conscious of school grades. Such a preoccupation militates against sheer quality of performance pursued for its own sake.

But at this point the impossibility of generalizing about the private secondary school reappears. For the best schools in the group are offering a course of study which they believe to be the most effective instrument for the achievement of the ends they have in view, among which college preparation is an important by-product. Students in such schools take the Board examinations in their stride and proverbially score higher than they do in their own secondary schools. Colleges recognize and make allowance for this fact. Any university or college admissions officer will give evidence that the grades reported and the recommendations submitted by schools presenting candidates for admission are by no means equally reliable; that the grades from certain schools must be heavily discounted in the prediction of collegiate success; and that in their comments on the qualifications of their candidates, some heads of schools chronically exaggerate the facts. The contention that private secondary schools operate under the pressure of the iron hand of college entrance requirements derives such substance as it has from the unquestionable truckling of inferior establishments.

The best private schools, however, are accustomed periodically to re-examine their curricula. For example, during the past few years the faculty over which I preside has made important changes in the requirements for graduation. None of them has been demanded or even suggested by the colleges. All of them have been intended to strengthen the quality of the school's academic training. The point of view that these schools do little more than pander to an entrenched collegiate hierarchy is ignorant and biased. And the charge that they do not "meet the real needs" of their students is an assertion without meaning in the absence of a definition of what "real needs" are.

Some schools express a measure of timidity toward the introduction of cultural pursuits in which the College Board offers no examinations or in which colleges are not accustomed to grant "credits." The credit or the unit system did at one time impose undue rigidity on preparatory courses of study. To the extent that it still does deprive candidates of the privilege of entering important fields of study which attract them, it is still to be condemned. But of recent years the situation has become much more flexible. Colleges today commonly approve the pursuit of whatever subjects have important relevance to higher education of a liberal arts or technical nature. They do specify minimum requirements in such subjects as are generally considered basic to higher education, as the only means of discovering whether candidates are prepared for it or not. No one would seriously urge upon them the acceptance of experimental preparatory programs which did not adequately test the basic aptitudes.

For the rest, the cry against credits and units would seem to be dying on the vine; and schools which complain that they can find no room or time for desirable academic interests beyond college entrance requirements may introduce them with the assurance that they will find collegiate favor if well done.

But since the public conviction of the inhibitory influence of college requirements dies hard, they need a word in defense of present procedures. In the first place, statistics accumulated over a long period indicate a close correlation between scores on the College Board Scholastic Aptitude Test and actual college freshman performance. They are not so reliable as grades at the school level, but they do apparently demonstrate that the test gives real distinction a chance to exhibit itself and that it rates candidates according to their proper places on the scale. In short, it does well precisely what it is intended to do.

In the second place, the so-called achievement tests are so devised that they neither require nor permit specific preparation, as the old subject-matter examinations used to do. They allow the schools, therefore, a wide freedom in choice of content and in methods of teaching. For example, the increasing practice of conducting all French instruction in French, and similarly with the other modern foreign languages, which is now spreading steadily in the schools, would have been impossible under the former type of Board examination, which stressed translation and grammar almost to the exclusion of speaking. Finally, schools sending large numbers of candidates to college every year have little fault to find with present evaluating procedures. Their experience is that, with few exceptions, colleges accept the candidates they ought to accept. Errors of judgment are rare. Colleges do not place undue importance on College

Board ratings. Schools which teach with faith and confidence material which they regard as intrinsically important may proceed without fear.

American schools, furthermore, under the pressure of securing college admission for all their students who want to go, are called upon to inform them frequently about how they are getting on along the path. The schools themselves need to know this too so that they can give reliable advice on the prospects of acceptance by the colleges preferred by their candidates. This gives rise in some schools to an overelaboration of quizzes, examinations, and grades, which unfortunately disposes students to concentrate on how well they are doing in comparison to their fellows rather than to their own maximum capacity. Some students, by a process of divination wholly ethereal, calculate the academic average to be required for entrance to a given college and rest when they have reached it. Even teachers are occasionally so unprofessional as to use this superstition as a goad to further effort, but only enough more, apparently, to meet the alleged need. One of the shortcomings of all this welter of piecemeal evaluation is that percentage grades or letters of the alphabet are not always a measure of real intellectual capacity. So-called objective tests, for example, if they are the kind that invite students to distinguish between true and false answers to a problem or to suggest which of five words is closest in meaning to a given word, have little to commend them except ease of administration and scoring. They may test the memory of facts or skill in guessing, and no teacher can possibly discover which it is. Certainly they have nothing to do with mental processes. The antidote within the schools is in common practice in the best of them: the construction of questions to which there are no "right" answers, which diagnose reliably and thoroughly the students' ability to make real use of the facts they have accumulated. A test which calls for the regurgitation of ill-digested gobbets of "knowledge" is not a test at all. Facts taught as facts are not a part of education. A store of facts is not knowledge. Knowledge is a grasp of the significance of facts. Good tests require the selection and the resynthesis of facts, their use in arriving at general conclusions. They should be so constructed as to permit the superior student to exhibit his superiority unmistakably. Finally, examinations should be regarded not as hurdles set up at intervals for boys and girls to stumble over, but as important instruments in the teaching process. For able young people, taking an examination ought to be a stimulating, interesting experience, demanding the best they have to give. They ought to know more at the end than they did at the beginning.

It is possible for students to begin to take this point of view as soon as teachers begin to emphasize it. If the goals of learning are kept constantly before students, if the real purpose of study is repeatedly stressed, if its relevance to individual need and experience is clarified, then the process becomes the mastery of principles rather than the memory of facts. When that point is reached, another characteristic affliction of American education can be relieved: its abnormal and unhealthy dread of examinations. In many college preparatory schools the approach of important examinations brings on terror and panic, visiting upon the school community that peculiarly American phenomenon, the cram session. Everybody knows that cramming is the worst possible way to fit the mind for its best performance, but nearly everybody does it. At the end of the senior year, when diplomas and graduation and honors lists and college admissions are all involved, I have seen final examinations cause worry, nervous tension, exhaustion, and sometimes an almost complete paralysis of the mental powers.

Responsibility for this frightening exhibition must rest in part upon our teachers. Though they do not mean to do so, it is they who create the atmosphere in which cramming seems to students to be essential. It is they, too, who make it possible. If students are encouraged to attend to their work regularly and if the meaning of its parts is made clear in the light of the whole, they ought to be ready for a test at any time, without the need of more than a brief review by way of preparation. A certain degree of nervous tension accompanies top performance in every kind of activity. It means that the glands are working and the faculties being sharpened. But when you see boys of the highest ability in a real state of funk for fear of failure, corrective measures would seem to be critically urgent.

But the fault may not fairly be laid on teachers in full. They are men under authority too, and they themselves deplore the condition to which they are in part contributing. The root of the difficulty, of which the culpability of schools is but a branch, is again the solid determination of their clientele to go to college. It is this urge which leads us to weight success in school so heavily on the side of academic proficiency, to the neglect of other estimable qualities of whose subtleties the adding-machine can give no account. And the final aggravation of the problem is the insistence of parents that their children not only go to college, but to the best colleges, by which they mean the colleges they think are socially superior. This preoccupation with prestige the forces of the time have in part circumvented. The sudden multiplication of the demand for college admission after the war increased competition for places in the "name" colleges, with the result that boys from private schools whose collegiate heart's desire would a few years earlier have been within their grasp were required to bestow their favor upon less highly touted institutions. Since most of them were also good institutions, the consequences proved to be happy for all concerned. But the pressure was always on the schools, and still is, to make the best of what often seemed to them a bad bargain; and one of the means they naturally used to stir boys into doing their best was to reiterate the importance of grades. Entrusted with students of enough ability to gain admission to a college, it was their responsibility to see that they got there.

They could obviously do more for such boys if they did not all propose to go to college, and probably do more for everybody from the top level of ability down. They could, for example, introduce greater flexibility of standards. As it is now, the college preparatory school applies the same standard of performance to everybody and holds everybody to the same minimum requirements in the different subject-matter fields. This is all very well for the purposes of students of reasonably versatile capacities. But there are many students at a lower level of academic aptitude whose powers are adequate for satisfactory work in certain subjects, but who in other fields stumble and grope and fail. If they are also commonplace in all other respects, they had better busy themselves in some more feasible pursuit. But often they are sound and admirable in character, faithful and responsible in the school community, the embodiment of all the moral virtues that it is the purpose of the schools to cultivate. When such young people fail and drop out, the waste in human values is great. In the face of the American obsession with college degrees it is difficult to stipulate any means of combating it which is likely to prove successful. Nevertheless, since character is the great end of the schools' efforts,

they ought not to resign themselves to relinquishing their
chance to educate a group of young people whose value as
citizens is potentially distinguished, just because they cannot
meet the requirements of the popular academic pattern. A
school is justified in setting store by its high standard of
academic performance, and there is no necessity of depressing
standards for the superior minority in order to accommodate
the lower ranges of intelligence. Every year, however, schools
give diplomas, signifying the successful completion of the
prescribed course of study, to students in whose soundness
as citizens they have little confidence. As they do so they
recall with sadness others, long since fallen by the wayside,
who they know will be useful and effective individuals all
their lives. The contrast is disturbing as well as ironic.

It ought to be possible for the schools to keep and train
young people whose effort is commendable, who are loyal
and influential as citizens, and who are evidently increasing
in stature under the schools' auspices. If the schools defined
those portions of the various fields of study which might
be regarded as the minimum that everyone must master who
hopes to lead a useful life, the sum would surely not exceed
the grasp of many; and it may be assumed that all students
in all private schools could go much further than the minimum
if the schools' offerings were sufficiently flexible. The idea
that educational values lie only in the course of study—or
even mainly there—is a limited and depressing one. And it
belies the experience of every people that among its strongest
leaders and its most important citizens there have been
many whose formal schooling has not proceeded through the
secondary level.

But even if they convince themselves that the liberal arts
curriculum contains values of unique importance to the
achievement of their ends, the private schools may not rest

there. Having decided that the material is good, they may not merely sit back and teach it. Their task is to see to it that its values get out of the textbooks and into the lives of the students. Otherwise they are merely displaying the dry bones of a cultural tradition which their students will regard as having supported at one time, perhaps, a structure of some antique elegance, but as bearing no relevance to the lives of men today. During the heyday of the classical curriculum, its supremacy lay not in the values it *contained* but in the fact that these values were *conveyed*; that they became the values of the men who studied them. No curriculum can in itself be virtuous. In a sense it can contain no moral value; for value is a term attached to something somebody does in comparison with something else which he might have done. Value becomes real only when it issues in action. If a man is taught a means of recognizing what is good, but neither cares about it nor does anything about it, he can scarcely be said to be educated. Education is not just a matter of how well a person learns a curriculum.

Today, however, it often seems as if it were. Every year a considerable number of boys and girls learn their curriculum pretty well and are complimented on it, though they be knaves and rogues at the end of the process. Prizes and honors generally recognize superior learning, which has nothing to do with honor; and candidates for awards intended to recognize high personal values are sometimes decried because they have not learned the curriculum well enough.

It is a general fact about our private schools that a wide gap separates the virtues and the values preached from those which campus life really practices, and one of the urgent tasks of such schools is to work toward closing the gap. In most schools the fabric of values is uneven and unclear. Too many values are accidental or unintended or undirected. Some of them are conflicting. Enterprises carelessly assumed to have educational implications or permitted to exist with or without them are too numerous. Campus life is over-organized. Meanwhile the schools' substantial agency of education, the course of study, does not seem to the average student to have vitality or urgency or to be connected with the pressing problems of the world he knows. That world is baffled and insecure, divided and perplexed by opposing ideologies. The life of schools in all its phases and in the sum total of its impact must find a way of imparting values firm enough and clear enough to carry men and women through their lives with faith and constancy.

The way does not necessitate the junking of the liberal arts curriculum. It is important, of course, that its contents be periodically re-examined from the standpoint of its effectiveness, both as knowledge and as a source of values, in equipping students to make discriminating decisions about the most important issues of life today. If parts of it do not appear to serve that end, they had better be taken out or else so radically revised in their presentation that they are restored to the central context. Many private schools would do well also to make wider use of methods and materials generally regarded as unconventional which would have the effect of illuminating the connection between what is being learned in the classroom and the problems of the world outside; for the academic profession is too prone to regard such divagations as unseemly or vulgar or unscholarly. There is little nourishment, on the other hand, in stampeding to the opposite extreme and importing curricular material simply because its bearing upon the present has an obvious immediacy, without regard for the values it may be supposed to convey.

The underlying need is simply stated, though its fulfillment be arduous and complicated. It is to see to it that the things students learn in the classroom are constantly and closely related to the rest of their school life. For nobody learns anything except by his personal experience, and it is unlikely that two people ever learn the same thing from the same experience. "Values themselves," says President Harold Taylor of Sarah Lawrence College, "have to be learned. But in order for values to be meaningful, and so absorbed into one's life as to have a continuing part in thought and in action, they must be learned as meaningful experience. The College community must therefore be organized so that each student is immersed in the stream of intellectual, social, and moral values which it is our intention to teach our youth. This means that we must have . . . more conscious effort to design a community in which each student and faculty member feels himself to be a part of a total enterprise in which he has a share and an important contribution to make. It is possible to create the same loyalty and enthusiasm for liberal values as the enthusiasm now reserved for football teams and fraternities." But, as President Taylor implies, the enthusiasm does have to be created; it will not come through hoping. Precisely the same challenge invites the secondary schools. To answer it is the business of a liberal education.

CHAPTER VIII

The Side Show

When Woodrow Wilson was president of Princeton he warned Princetonians that the side show was threatening to submerge the operations in the main tent; that the thought and time and energy devoted to "extracurricular activities" were distracting undergraduates from the vigorous pursuit of intellectual disciplines that was the university's chief concern.

For many years the same distortion of values has been a conspicuous feature of campus life in the private schools. A school's academic program is a carefully constructed instrument for the achievement of stated ends. It functions under systematic scrutiny and controls. When it is altered, the purpose is to make it a more effective instrument. In the provision of various nonacademic activities, too, schools theoretically are equally concerned that their strictly educational possibilities shall be clearly formulated and carefully guided, and the results rigorously evaluated. Opportunities for self-development should obviously be diverse in recognition of widely different student interests and capacities. Curricular and extracurricular activity, that is to say, are not inherently in conflict or opposition if the notion is accepted that "curriculum" includes everything a child does in a school, not merely his course of study. They are merely different phases of a single educational plan. In fact, however, "extracurricular activity" does often appear to be in competition with the plan of studies instead of a supplement to it. Private schools, free to control their whole environments, may be expected to take the lead in resolving the dilemma.

It is not hard to see why the "side show" is seductive.

In the first place, it offers, in contrast to the compulsion of the classroom, the attraction of the voluntary. What a man does because he wants to is done for fun; it is a means of recreation, refreshment, and relief; and he is likely to work harder at it, to put more of his real best into it, than into projects which, because they are imposed upon him, may seem laborious and grinding.

In the second place, the rewards of extracurricular activity are of short range, easily perceived and soon won. The athlete, the editorial writer, the singer, the popular leader are placed under discipline, to be sure; but their travail is brief, their achievement readily and quickly recognized, their release from strain tolerably close.

Finally, and most important, the successful pursuit of extracurricular position endows the winner with prestige and prominence. It brings glory with it. It gratifies the ego. These are not in themselves discreditable incentives. It is a good thing for everyone to test his powers against those of others and, after stiff competition, come out ahead. For a shy or diffident child, such an experience may well mean the birth of self-confidence. The trouble is that, human nature being what it is, action may be so completely motivated by the desire to be conspicuous for its own sake that the opportunity for excellence is forgotten in the satisfaction of being merely better than someone else. It is hard to stop boys, at least—

and perhaps girls too—from "going out" for things in the interest of rounding up the longest possible list of items for the yearbook; and the typical campus "big shot" is on the whole an unattractive person, conscious of everything about himself except his limitations.

The Yale Institute of Human Relations was founded to enlist the services of scientists in several fields in the study of the problems of man as a social animal and to synthesize their findings. When its purposes were still not clearly understood by the public, a young man was taking an afternoon stroll in New Haven with the lady whose favor he was presently eager to secure. "What is that building over there?" she asked. "That," he replied, "is the Institute of Human Relations." "What do they do there?" she pressed. "I'm not quite sure," he answered; "but whatever it is, they do it together." The dominance of the machinery of "activities" on school campuses is due in part to an apparently insatiable American appetite for doing things together. When two boys discover that they like to play chess, the local culture is not congenial to their merely playing chess together. It suggests the insertion in the school paper of a notice advertising the time and place of a meeting of all boys interested in the organization of a chess club, with officers and dues, the latter for the provision of refreshments after the battle has cleared. One argument for the encouragement of special inclinations is to provide means of diversion, for the indulgence of hobby riding in moments of leisure. The American nature, however, is inclined to disapprove of the ensnarements of leisure as constituting inducements to moral flaw; Wordsworth's "wise passiveness" is abhorrent to it. The amateur spirit is the pose of the dilettante. "Activities" are the refuge against the abyss of aloneness, of lack of occupation. It is doubtful that, in their lives at school, American girls and boys are overworked. It is appallingly certain that they are overbusy.

Somehow the side show has got out of hand. Surely our schools may not petulantly frown upon it or harshly suppress it in the interests of "education." It *is* education. It simply needs intelligent direction and control. It needs the cultivation within the school management of a clear definition of what it is a school is trying to do in the round, and of the contribution each part of the sum is intended and designed to furnish. The fault is a lack of proportion. The school's object is to provide each student with a coherent experience, its parts related to each other, its balance thoughtfully contrived. At present too many lives are cut up into little pieces, without reason or meaning; too much time is frittered away in agitated doing.

The conviction that extracurricular activities are a distraction from the purposes of education, rather than a means of realizing them, is a delusion of adult minds. A familiar pedagogical point of view maintains that academic concerns alone are educational and advocates the strict curbing of all other occupations as a necessary precaution against the seductions of the frivolous and trivial. Teachers of this frame of mind customarily believe that students whose academic performance is unsatisfactory should be barred from extracurricular participation until they have shown signs of true repentance and mended their ways. No doubt egregious loafers must be summarily dealt with, and some students, in the absence of the counsel and guidance they may properly suppose their school should offer, will satiate themselves at the extracurricular table to their own chronic indigestion.

Generally speaking, however, the prohibitory treatment errs in two respects. First, as has been said, it implicitly denies that nonacademic activities contain educational values, labeling them as diversionary. Second, it embraces the notion that, if a student is forbidden to participate in projects which he evidently enjoys and from which he is apparently deriving, in marked degree, the satisfaction of successful accomplishment, he will turn to his studies with new heart and energy. It seems more probable that agreeable achievement in a naturally attractive field will put a student, if he is wisely admonished, in better mind to attack the duties of the classroom. In the broad view, at any rate, the problem of "competitive" interests approaches a solution once it is conceded that the "curriculum" embraces everything that happens to a student in school and that each part of it, therefore, ought to be designed, conducted, and appraised in the light of its basic educational values.

Stated unqualifiedly, this dictum gives rise to the horrid picture of teachers assiduously going about watching students doing things, drawing moral inferences, frowning on frivolity and lack of earnestness. That would be folly twice compounded. The praise of idleness has been admirably sung by Robert Louis Stevenson, and every schoolteacher should tune his voice to it. The fruits of inactivity may nourish and sustain, however thin the soil that corporate bustle may supply. Zealous teachers are wont to forget that the appearance of indolence may signify illumination rather than delinquency; or to forget, wanting in charity, that it may signify merely indolence, which every youth should turn to at times as a blessed refuge from the concerted attempts of his elders to improve him. To go through a day or two now and then without learning anything revives one's tolerance for edification.

The point is that every exercise *to which a school gives form* should be a part of a concerted whole, to be kept in its place, directed toward its purpose, and guarded from distortion and exaggeration.

Athletic games are a case in point, since they are far and away the most richly burgeoning exhibit in the academic side show. Curators of the young, both professional and lay, commonly deplore the distortions of American "overemphasis on athletics." Their compunction is misdirected. Nearly all young people have a natural proclivity for games, which they play instinctively and irresistibly, even if they have to make them up. If the games give range to the display of physical prowess, so much the more avid their pursuit. In a sense, schools *could* not emphasize athletics. They emphasize themselves. In the minds of girls and boys they are a part of the very nature of things; without them life would be stunted and lopsided. All this is as it should be, and mentors need not disturb themselves about it.

The proper object of their attack is American overemphasis on athleticism, which is the exploitation of the star. The star system in American colleges and universities has been condoned and frequently encouraged by higher institutions which, mistrusting the power of intellectual distinction to arrest the public mind, have lapsed into the suspicion that their reputations will languish unless they can be substantiated by the self-evident impressiveness of winning teams. The glittering paraphernalia of stadiums, subsidized players, highly paid coaches, box-office receipts—and alumni committees on athletics—are the easily predictable consequences of an unseemly ·scholarly timidity. And not only unseemly, but contrary to the facts. Eagerness to attend the best colleges and universities—best in point of academic standards—varies not one whit in reaction to the ebb and flow of their athletic fortunes. The University of Chicago remains important without a football team. Great athletic performances are universally and properly admired. They contain in themselves no obstacles to learning. It is only when athleticism is allowed to career along its own merry way, its potential virtues insubordinate to a general plan of education, that it becomes a monster.

The method schools should use, then, is not to suppress it but to control it; to give it its proper place but no more; to prune its excrescences and hold it to a true and healthy growth.

If schools regard football, for example, as a desirable exercise for male youth, it ought to be taught as well as history or science is taught. Requirements for coaches ought to be the same as for all other instructors: scholarship, personality, and character. In performance, too, they should be held to the same criteria of satisfaction: superior grounding in their subject; the ability to expound it skillfully and intelligibly; a continuing eagerness to keep abreast with fresh developments.

To some observers these stipulations suggest the odor of professionalism. When they say that games should be played for their own sake, they are right; but they do not mean the same thing as when they say that poetry should be studied for its own sake. They entertain the misgiving that the serious cultivation of excellence in any game turns it into a crusade instead of a recreation and somehow repudiates the creed of amateur sportsmanship. It is difficult to believe, however, that the amiable duffer derives more pleasure from his exertions than the accomplished performer; and the notion that a game is just as much fun, however well or badly it is played, belies the general experience.

If, as occasionally happens, schoolboys come to regard football as the highest good that an otherwise impoverished life can offer, and defeat as the ultimate in dust and ashes, the fault lies not in the ideal of excellence but in the extravagant representations of the coaches; in other words, in poor teaching; which deserves the same corrective measures that would be applied to a teacher of science who affirmed that the discoveries of physics invalidated the claims of religion. The coach and the teacher, having both wandered out of bounds, would have to be put back again. Beyond the occasional need for checking such normal exuberance, schools should see to it that good games are well taught—as well taught as any other part of the curriculum.

If schools regard coaches as important members of the teaching staff, as they should, they must bear with them in moments of adversity. Interest in victory, to be sure, is universal. A school senior, addressing an assembly of his fellow students, explored the strategy and tactics of the Battle of Chancellorsville with admirable mastery and evoked acute questions from both boys and teachers—of which the most penetrating was propounded by a small sixth-grader who, just before the bell rang, asked who won. He had expressed the common concern. All teams want to win, and most of them try to. Yet as long as a coach teaches well and his team plays as well as it has been taught, defeat should not be allowed to besmirch his reputation. He should feel that his position is secure. When a football player is guilty of stupidity, voices are frequently raised to blame the lapse on the coach—a misconception which a brief review of the process of heredity would dissolve. If the same boy is stupid in his mathematics class, public opinion arrives at the more charitable assumption that his limitation is his private cross, and his teacher's withers are unwrung. Yet in some schools coaches are made to feel that they must win or go; or at least that they fall somehow short of full professional respectability. The effect upon them is ignominious and humiliating.

If a coach proves to be a poor teacher, the case is different. Given students of sufficient ability, classroom teachers may properly be expected to bring them to a point of competence consistent with the school's standards. The same result should be expected of a coach. But just as no classroom teacher would be held to the same degree of success with a mediocre group as with a superior one, so a coach should be judged by how much he accomplishes with the material at his disposal and not merely by his record of victories.

This reasonable stipulation is so obvious that there should be no need to mention it. Athletics, however, and particularly football, proceed in an atmosphere of emotional and nervous agitation. They cannot be approached with academic calm. As public spectacles they have an explosive effect upon public opinion. Especially in the larger and older boarding schools, excitable and sclerotic alumni, their former prowess suffering no abatement in the comforting vagaries of nostalgic reverie, identify defeat with a general decadence of stamina in modern youth and address moral exhortations to headmasters. It behooves schools, therefore, to keep constantly before their membership the ideals and the advantages of sports in education and to check extravagances with cool head and firm hand.

The danger that exceptional athletes will be apotheosized has led some schools to give up interscholastic play altogether, in the conviction that the urge to win inevitably overwhelms the purposes of true sport. But it need not be so; the remedy is more drastic than the problem requires. Old rivalries between two schools do sometimes give rise to undesirable emotional tension in teams and students; but coaches and teachers, if they take note and care, can keep it within bounds. Beyond that and on the positive side, interscholastic contests bring to a school a heightened consciousness of unity and corporate identity. The enthusiastic support of a team by its schoolmates strengthens the general morale through its evidence of institutional solidarity, its enlistment of everybody in a cause which has vivid and picturesque reality and which transcends selfish interests. Proverbially the first football game of a school year pulls a school together, makes it feel for the first time that it is a school, with a relatively glorious past and, if the game is won, an illimitable future. It introduces "we" into the undergraduate vocabulary.

But football, despite its supremacy in the hierarchy of athletic glory, is an item only in a school's design for physical education, and school teams in every field deserve only the notice and prestige that follow upon their superior proficiency.

The first object of physical education is to endow each student with the degree of physical proficiency that his natural equipment permits. The aim here is not to make an accomplished athlete of him, but to make him reasonably able-bodied. His particular needs should be determined by careful examination, and appropriate exercises should be prescribed to meet them. If a student is ill coordinated or awkward, and especially if he is shy and self-conscious because of his deficiencies, the training provided for him and others like him should serve to bring him along to a point of development where he will begin to have confidence in himself.

The need for specialized exercise is not limited to children of low physical caliber. Good athletes frequently profit by the bolstering of minor weaknesses, and good coaches of all sports impose upon their squads developmental techniques particularly aimed at their muscular requirements.

Within the field of remedial exercise today, the inculcation of good posture enjoys an energetic vogue. Sway-backed, droop-shouldered children, if parental anxiety can be relied on, are increasing in numbers with alarming rapidity. When parents discuss their hopes for the contribution a school may make to the enlightenment of their offspring, the insistence that they be taught how to stand up straight appears with singular emphasis.

It is a tall order to fill. The implication of it is that schools are privy to secret formulas enabling them to solve the puzzle to which parents themselves, having had control of their children during their formative years, while all the damage was being done, have been denied access. Strictly speaking, it is impossible to make anybody stand up straight. Also, up to the age at which vanity can no longer rely on the support of the abdominal muscles, people can stand up straight whenever they feel like it. Silhouette photographs of children, therefore, before and after posture training, are of more interest pictorially than therapeutically, since normal abandon can be resumed as soon as the lens has clicked. The only contribution which physical training can make to the current epidemic is the establishment of a degree of sound musculature, the normal consequence of which is that its beneficiaries will be likely to stand straight anyway.

Modern theory prescribes that the achievement of physical proficiency should make wide use of games. The old regime of Indian clubs and chest weights, of parallel bars and push-ups, still has auxiliary values, but its employment as a steady diet is obsolete. It used to consign the physically inefficient—"P.I.'s," as physical directors scornfully called them—to the perennial ignominy of failure, and public failure at that, in their futile attempts to pass the tests required for participation in team sports; and the work was drudgery pure and simple, with no incentive and no fun.

Under the present happier order, intramural games become an especially valuable medium of education. That framework of physical education is best which offers each boy and girl an opportunity to play on a team representing a group which has genuine standing in the school community, so that to play for it is an accomplishment which receives public recognition. Such an arrangement gives everybody, at his own level of ability, the same kind of satisfaction that members of school teams receive. And only team play can bring to the surface the instinctive individual responses to competitive physical effort that teachers and coaches must notice and influence if sport is to be made a means of education as well as of pleasure and physical expression. Intramural sport presents the additional advantage that, by providing competition for all degrees of skill, size, and stamina, it does not press a child beyond his strength and therefore run the risk of overexertion and strain.

The by-products of athletic competition compose a kind of moral training of first importance to a school's purposes. The subordination of emotion in the interests of a mental and physical coordination is a lesson best learned through team play. So is the concept that in any corporate effort the quixotism of the prima donna is intolerable. These are benefits which school faculties should wish to support and encourage, for they become a part of personality and character, affecting all behavior, influencing accomplishment on every side.

Finally, games as pure recreation can be lifelong assets, for which schools should prepare as systematically as they train for team play. Such individual accomplishments as golf, tennis, other court games, and swimming have an importance as carry-over skills which the superior prestige of contact sports should not be permitted to eclipse. Ten years out of college the football player can only jaw about his game. The golfer can still play it. A combination of the two serves as an outlet for both anecdote and action.

One American headmaster, after two years in office, feels that in our private boarding schools "we get so preoccupied with getting our daily chores done that we give little time to long-range thinking, and in addition are inclined against new ideas if only for the reason that they usually mean more work, when we already have, we think, more than we can handle."

Another touches on the same problem in different words when he says that we are too much concerned with the by-products of the educational process: that we are unduly gratified by the appearance of hard work and decent behavior; that our machinery of plans and systems uses up too much of our time and energy. What we need to increase, he continues, is our practice of direct character training, the systematic and deliberate cultivation of values.

The justice of these admonitions is exhibited by the array of organizations and activities, outside the areas of study and athletics, which most of our schools supply. All of them contain intrinsic merit, offering opportunities for recreational, cultural, or creative expression. The trouble is that too few students receive their benefits. Art, music, journalistic and imaginative writing, dramatics, shopwork, and other such pursuits all have their place in a program of liberal education. As such, they deserve to be within the reach of everybody instead of organized for the few. They attract the gifted spontaneously, and one of the encouraging developments in the private schools during the past decade has been the extraordinary elevation in the quality of musical, literary, and artistic production. Yet because they are commonly regarded as "extracurricular," and therefore apart from the main busi-

ness of "education," most schools sandwich them in at odd
and frequently inadequate and inconvenient periods; and
students who are in scholastic difficulties are generally denied
the opportunity to enjoy them at all. A chronic complaint in
our schools, indeed, is the impossibility of "finding time"
for matters of conceded merit. And some teachers frown
upon projects of extraordinary educational value on the
grounds that they take students away from their studies and
occasionally interfere with the preparation of classroom as-
signments.

There ought not to be such a state of affairs and could
not be if faculties of schools were to re-examine their convictions about what a liberal education, broadly viewed,
should contain and then distribute the available time among
the various approved fields. No teacher would be likely to
hold that the content of a liberal education and the content
of a classroom course of study were identical—not, at least,
if he were thinking of values as well as knowledge.

The first result of such a re-examination would be that
such present activities as were considered particularly desirable as parts of a total educational experience would be made
legitimate and respectable by inclusion in the school calendar.
The second and almost equally important result would be
that all the rest of the top-heavy machinery of organized
busyness would be thrown aside. Here again a leaf from the
book of English practice deserves our reading. In the English public school there are far fewer activities than in America; but the ones that do exist are far more numerously
patronized and enjoy the respect and the participation of
the whole school community.

Such a rearrangement of the place of cultural pursuits in
our educational plan would be likely to develop an interesting
change in their public reputation. In American schools today,

for example, the traditional consignment of music and literature to the shadowy limbo of spare-time diversions makes it difficult to get voluntary student attendance at concerts and lectures. Students are likely to shy away from such occasions on the ground that they constitute a reprehensible adult attempt to "put over" culture on them; or that public attendance on such dubious proceedings will mark them as exotic or precious; or merely because of indifference or boredom. And if attendance is compelled, they are likely to protest at what they regard as an unfair intrusion upon their "free time," in which they may properly anticipate relaxing to the level of mental torpor from which they seem to believe they derive the greatest comfort. It is unfortunately true that many teachers are similarly unresponsive, though occasionally for different reasons. No one ought to expect that students will pay serious attention to provisions for entertainment or enlightenment which a school's adult population evidently regards as a chore beyond the line of duty. If the arts and crafts, however, had full standing and general prominence and support, young people, always likely to respond to the values they see are genuinely cherished, might perhaps be expected to take advantage of their cultivating influence.

For they are an excellent medium for the forming of taste and style, particularly since they call for the active contribution of the individual student rather than for the passive receptivity with which he sometimes approaches his classroom work. In the direction of such activities, therefore, teachers should bear in mind that it is the students' taste that is to be developed, not teachers' taste that is to be imposed. There are schools whose literary magazines and newspapers are subjected to faculty censorship down to the last comma, adjective, and human situation, so that they become a record of adult respectability rather than of undergraduate skill, lucidity, and imagination.

In such a field as music, of course, a discipline must be imposed first; the mechanics of producing sound must be established; after which the growth of taste and appreciation may go on apace. The case of painting is the same, though here the teacher must be careful to give the student the means of accomplishing his own ideas, however unattractive they may appear to be to his instructor. But in the pursuit of writing, taste will be developed more effectively if young authors are left a good deal alone, and the adverse criticism of their lapses from propriety should be based on the appropriateness of their expression, on its artistic necessity or integrity, rather than on the apprehension that they will flutter the nerves and agitate the scruples of adult readers. The literary and journalistic poseur who aims to shock, the dealer in snigger and innuendo, can scarcely be won over by the stipulation that his taste is offensive. He knows that and likes it. It is easier to approach him with the supposition that he wants to be a serious writer and to lead him to the recognition that he is a poor one. If there are present in a faculty men or women who are able not only to teach literature but to produce it, their example will be a power in the inculcation of standards among their pupils. Freedom of speech and expression must sometimes be modified, to be sure, in the interests of the reputation of a school, for the cultivation of sound taste cannot be achieved in the absence of an awareness that it has limits and involves responsibilities. In general, however, the excesses it occasionally produces are probably less damaging, educationally speaking, than their prevention by adult edict.

There is room in our private schools, where directed

experimentation is easily possible, for a unifying process of cultural training that would give place and relevance to the whole range of intellectual, aesthetic, spiritual, and physical objectives which humane men have sought to reach.

CHAPTER IX

"You Are the Light of the World"

One of the purposes most frequently avowed by private schools is that of training leaders. In fact, they not only avow the purpose: they often affirm its accomplishment. Now, the purpose itself is admirable: the American democracy needs intelligent, devoted leadership, and education is perhaps the chief instrument (certainly the most obvious one) by which it may be provided. And the duty of schools in this pursuit is the more imperious in a day when the influence of church and family is no longer so potent as it used to be. Often, however, schools fall into error in the concepts and the methods they conceive to achieve their purpose. About the qualities that should constitute leadership they are frequently vague and sometimes sentimental; and when they undertake the task of designating students who embody their ideals they are likely to go all out for the conventional, if not the commonplace.

The fact is, of course, that you cannot make leaders; you can only recognize them and try to guide them to lead soundly. And even these more modest ends are hard to reach. For not only is it impossible to make leaders; it is also impossible to prevent them; and this poses a problem. For all teachers remember boys and girls whose qualities of leadership were so formidable, not to say incorrigible, that they led themselves right out of school by way of dismissal. The poet Shelley was dismissed from Oxford not because he was brilliant, but because his religious views were unconventional and inconvenient; and those today who visit the Shelley memorial at University College are entitled to wonder precisely what it celebrates. In their responsibility for recognizing leadership, school faculties should be tolerant, perceptive, and long-suffering. Similarly it is not easy to say what makes leadership "sound." It is tempting to affirm that sound leadership in a school may be defined as the sort of leadership that the faculty itself considers sound. In the end, it has to be that, of course. Standards must be set; instruments of measurement must be devised; and the faculty must provide them. But here again school faculties, perplexed and harassed by adolescent perversities, are likely (with some excuse for it) to identify the sound with the convenient or the satisfactory. What teachers describe as a "thoroughly satisfactory" girl or boy is likely to be a person who does the academic task well and breaks no rules—a sort of negative and uninviting paragon. To recognize and train leaders, men and women need humility, imagination, humanity, and, above all, faith.

You cannot contribute to the training of leaders, as almost all private schools are prone to do, by repeatedly telling boys and girls that they are going to be leaders and that therefore they have special responsibilities. Such admonitions are intended to stimulate the conscience. All too frequently they elevate the ego. Instead of stimulus they encourage smugness. They permit the comforting assurance that, since positions of leadership are theirs by birth or circumstance, their privileges are more important than their responsibilities. To some students, furthermore, to be told over and over again that they are potential leaders has a chilling or numbing effect which produces a temporary atrophy of their initiative and may develop into a chronic indifference. Others it irritates.

I suspect that there is no aspect of a school's objectives to which precept is less relevant and useful than in this matter of leadership. Most boys and girls of high school age are not eagerly responsive to general and long-range appeals. They react to the specific and the immediate. Schools need badly to remember this in formulating and executing their plans for leadership training.

General exhortations along the "You are the salt of the earth," "You are the light of the world" line have the further and damning defect that they are not true. Most boys and girls are simply not going to be leaders, and it is not merely harmful but also dishonest to tell them that they are. On the basis of a wide acquaintance with boys of high school age, to many of whom I am devoted, my assurance that most of them would not be leaders I have often regarded as a dispensation, from which I have derived both comfort and relief. Most boys and girls are going to be followers; and it is the business of our schools to try to make them well informed, discriminating, conscientious, and faithful followers. All who come to them the private schools must seek to enlighten and to temper, so that, whatever positions they may later occupy, they may be able to withstand in the evil day, and having done all, to stand. But they must not be miscast.

Another common error is to tell children that school is a preparation for life. This blunder is notoriously committed by Commencement orators who, pressed by the burden of adult responsibilities which their education has not prepared them to sustain, reassure themselves by the delusion that the pains and the problems of growing up are trivial and amusing.

"These school days are the happiest time of your lives," they declare. The remark is stupid and obtuse—and wrong.

The fact is that school days, far from being the easiest, are the most difficult period in the life of an individual, at least potentially and often actually. The reason is not hard to see. Adults visiting a school campus proverbially comment on its air of happiness. Indeed it is superficially happy. There is a lot of fun in it. But the adult should not deceive himself. Beneath the surface of multiform activity every high school girl or boy is wrestling with the problem of growing up, of making a satisfactory adjustment to adulthood. No one goes through this struggle without pain and failure and discouragement and fear and disillusionment. And some boys find the worry and the perplexity too much for them, and they break under them. In such a situation, too much preoccupation with training for leadership is premature. The first task is to train for wholeness, for a sense of adequacy and self-confidence.

And the place to do it is in the school and through the life of the school, which is the only life of which the individual girl or boy is a member. Children are members of a family life too, of course, and some of them have a church life. But so do their mothers and fathers. The point is that school life is the only life in which the child is engaged on his own, not as a member of a family, but as himself. School for him is his private domain, in which no other member of his family has a stake. It is his individual world, in the same sense in which his father's business or profession and his mother's homemaking are theirs. The child feels it to be so, and wants it to be recognized as so. It is of the greatest importance to a child's development that parents and teachers should so regard it.

No one could doubt this who has seen boys at a boarding school on the occasion of a visitation by fathers or mothers.

In a sense, the descent of parents on a school is regarded by their offspring as an intrusion, just as adults, unable naturally or tactfully or comfortably to absorb children into their group, often, after a period of constraint or specious camaraderie, suggest that they be off on their own concerns. This is generally a relief to the children. It seems too bad, therefore, that, the amenities of family life being what they are, children cannot also bid their parents "run along now" when they too have outworn their welcome. This sense of private worlds, so important to everybody's need for a consciousness of personal identity, of personal importance, has nothing to do with any absence of congeniality or lack of devotion among the members of a family. It is the common requirement of human personality. It is both entertaining and encouraging, therefore, to see boys showing parents about their school: enlightening their ignorance, admonishing their blunders, shuddering at their gaucheries, anticipating and diverting their ineptitudes—and all this with pride and affection, and with an exhilarating, normal, and entirely proper elevation of the ego.

Since the private schools are free to select as pupils whom they wish and to do with them what they will, they may, if they are wise enough, establish social ends which they consider desirable for every child and devise a pattern of life calculated to serve those ends.

In this process of formulating ends and means, the training of leaders is by no means inconsiderable. But it is a task for self-effacing men and women. For the recognition of potential leadership is by no means synonymous with its proper guidance. It is necessary for a school to decide what moral qualities a leader should possess, what sort of leadership he is intended to exert, and whom he is expected to lead. Teachers themselves occupy positions of leadership. They may set a bad example by exerting their authority capriciously, irritably, or arbitrarily. They may unconsciously regard it as desirable that their pupils grow up to be like themselves. In setting standards and measuring progress, therefore, they must make an effort to transcend their own limitations; and, as adults, they must exercise charity toward girls and boys whose mistakes they could probably avoid, but whose essential possibilities may lie beyond their reach.

Those who hope to train leaders must avoid another pitfall. Americans are prone to identify leadership with prominence. On our school and college campuses position counts. Honors are likely to be awarded to the conspicuous rather than to the superior. The athlete is widely admired; not, to be sure, without some reason. Physical prowess and stamina are enviable assets. They are usually accompanied by assurance and self-confidence: qualities common among people who are good at games. Naturally they inspire confidence. They also suggest a capacity for leadership which may not in reality exist. In consequence, athletes are frequently elected to offices whose responsibilities they are ill fitted to perceive. In the English public schools, the top scholar in a house is commonly appointed head of the house. The results, I am told, are highly satisfactory. There is in the English schools plenty of what in this country is called "overemphasis on athletics." Yet the English, in providing leadership for the school community, evidently have more confidence in brains than we do. It is not a tradition which would find nourishing soil in American schools, and certainly we should not do well to imitate it outright. It is perhaps instructive, however, for us to bear it in mind as we formulate the qualities of leadership that we think should be fostered and recognized in our training for American citizenship.

I have said that the first task of our schools is to train for wholeness, for a sense of adequacy and self-confidence; and that the place to do it is in the school and through the life of the school. The duty of a school is not to try, directly and deliberately, to make a child a leader. It is to give him a feeling of belonging to his group, of occupying a definite, recognized niche in the common life; not necessarily a prominent place, but one which feeds adequately his need for recognition and self-realization. And you cannot do this by giving him authority or privileges. You can do it only by giving him responsibility—and responsibility *within the life of the school.* For the success of a school in training for citizenship rests not in the number of conspicuous leaders it graduates, but in the degree to which it has implanted a sense of responsibility to the school community in each of its members, whether they have been conspicuous or not.

The instrument designed and directed for the fulfillment of this need is usually some form of "student government."

I find the term inaccurate, misleading, and objectionable. I know of no school in which the students do all the governing, and I should consider such a situation not only alarming but immoral. I do know of schools in which I think they do altogether too much of it. The practice of schools in regard to student participation in administration varies enormously between widely separated extremes. Sometimes there is little or none, all decisions being made by the faculty or, in a few instances, by the head of the school. At the opposite extreme, sometimes student groups are given unqualified authority to make all decisions bearing upon student life, including the authority to dismiss other students. Most schools occupy an intermediate ground.

I find a tendency among teachers and students alike to believe that the more student government there is, the better the school. I consider it an unprincipled belief, for the reason that the management of a group, whatever the field of its activity, ought to be based on the division and assignment not of authority but of responsibility. The assignment of full disciplinary authority to a student group is a denial of this principle. There are practical objections to it too, of course: the exercise of full authority by students may become capricious, autocratic, and tyrannical (a tendency from which faculties also are not immune). It is necessarily inexperienced, and therefore peculiarly prone to faulty judgment and inconsistency. Finally, it is likely to be intolerant and too severe. But the chief objection to it is that it ignores the fundamentally important distinction between authority and responsibility.

For in a school the handling of major disciplinary problems is not the responsibility of students; it is the responsibility of the head of the school. This is inherent in the nature of the relationship between a school and its patrons. When a child is to be enrolled in a school, the parent is responsible for making the application, not the child; and the head of the school is responsible for his admission, not the student council. The parent and the head are the contracting parties, and they are the only parties qualified to undertake responsibility in the matter. If it becomes necessary, as it occasionally does, to dismiss a child from a school, the same two contracting parties are again involved, and nobody else, as far as responsibility is concerned. The head is responsible to the parents, not the students to the parents.

When a student is elected to office by his fellows— whether to a captaincy, an editorship, or to membership on a council—he is not by their intention being given authority; he is being given responsibility. They are voting for him to take charge of something; and they are tacitly voting him such authority—and no more—as he must possess if he is to carry out his responsibility. Authority is valuable only as an instrument for the execution of responsibility.

At the end of a spring term in a boys' boarding school, two boys were nominated for the presidency of their respective houses. One boy refused the nomination. He said the office would require him to judge and sometimes to punish his housemates; that he was unwilling to do this, believing that as a matter of principle no boy was qualified to judge his fellows; that as a matter of practice the administration of discipline ought to be in the hands of the faculty, of whom, apparently, nothing better could be expected; and that certain forms of behavior which he would be supposed to censure did not seem to him objectionable. In short, he declined to undertake a responsibility which his convictions would not permit him to carry out. Some of those who had nominated him urged him to accept election, assume the honor, and let come what might. From the adult standpoint, having regard for the boy's unusual qualities of leadership, it seemed regrettable that he was unwilling to accept a responsibility for which he was so exceptionally fitted. On the other hand, it was impossible not to respect his honesty and candor.

The other presidential nominee held the same views, but did not declare them. He accepted the office with unstated reservations. He wanted the honor, not unnaturally. He enjoyed the prominence and the authority, which on occasion he enforced. But he repudiated the responsibility. Before his year in office was over, he was thoroughly discredited.

A senior council once reported to me an offense committed by one of their classmates for which the penalty was usually dismissal, recited all the circumstances, and recommended that he be expelled. I felt that the recommendation was just and responsible. When I reached my office the next morning, however, and before I had had time to interview the offender,

I found waiting for me an impressive delegation of his classmates who, though they confirmed his offense, declared that
certain members of the council who had voted for his dismissal had themselves committed the same offense repeatedly.
I found this declaration to be true. This revelation put the
council's noses out of joint, of course, and they finished the
year in the odor of public repudiation. But it is the aftermath
of the episode that is instructive. One of the offending council members, who had cast his vote for dismissal, told me, in
apparently sincere perplexity, that he had supposed it was
his duty to enforce the rules rather than observe them; and
I was given the impression that in some way I had let the
council down and consigned them to general and undeserved
humiliation by not carrying out their recommendation
promptly and with no questions asked. The incident was an
eloquent example of what can happen in a school when
authority is placed in the hands of irresponsible individuals. It
led to a thorough review of the objectives and the operation
of student government within the school.

Student "government," or any other kind of government,
emphasizes authority. In its place I advocate a plan of school
management which gives to students prescribed *responsibilities*, and only enough authority to execute them. And in
dealing with young people, the responsibilities assigned to
any group should be strictly limited to those for which the
group expresses an unqualified willingness to be responsible.
You cannot fairly hold them to implied responsibilities to
which they have made no commitment. You cannot talk
vaguely about trust and honor and the code of gentlemen. No
adult would accept responsibility in the absence of a precise
clarification of its terms. There is no reason why girls and
boys of high school age should be expected to behave differ-
ently. I should rather, therefore, have a group assume a

limited responsibility, far below my expectation or hope, and live up to it, than to imply their acceptance of a larger share and then repudiate a part of it. It is the part of the adult members of a school community to encourage the acceptance by student groups of an increasing measure of undergraduate responsibility, but the process must be specific and step by step. I am a little tired of hearing students told that they have disappointed hopes which have never been made clear to them.

In emphasizing the importance of a clear definition of group responsibilities, I do not mean that irresponsibility in areas not included in the definition should be condoned. You cannot teach responsibility by the book, and "It doesn't say you have to" or "It doesn't say you can't" is not an admissible excuse for oversight or negligence. The exercise of responsibility involves the exercise of judgment, which cannot be confined to verse and chapter. I am merely remarking that anyone is more likely to do his best when he knows exactly what is expected of him.

The proper management of a school is in essence the performance of a large number of responsibilities of various degrees of importance. They cannot be performed unless they are distributed. Their distribution involves the head of the school, the faculty, and the students. You do not begin by deciding *how much* responsibility should be given to each. You begin by deciding *what* responsibilities they should receive. And they should receive those responsibilities which, by virtue of their position in the school, they are naturally and evidently best fitted to discharge. You make each of them responsible for what they are closest to, for what they know all about, for what they live with, for what they can most promptly and easily handle. In other words, you establish spheres of responsibility, and you define their limits carefully. You have respect for each other's spheres, and you do not encroach upon them—a compunction which, I fear, some teachers are less likely to observe than students. Within your own sphere, your responsibility and your authority are absolute. When your sphere overlaps another's, your responsibility is contingent and your authority shared; and a solution is arrived at by conference. You keep out of each other's way, but everybody works together.

All systems of school administration which involve the participation of students are subjected to the criticism that they restrict opportunities for leadership to a few. Some schools, therefore, advocate the occupancy of positions of leadership in rotation, so that everybody gets a chance to lead. The notion is ingenious, and it appears to satisfy the demands of an evenhanded justice—which is not interested in leadership and is also proverbially blind. For the scheme is sentimental and unrealistic. The criticism can be met by seeing to it that everybody in a school is given a definite responsibility which is recognized and respected. Beyond that, it is dangerous and mawkish to juggle with the fact that some girls and boys are better in the top jobs than others. Those in minor positions should be made to feel that their contributions to the common life are valuable and indispensable; but it does them no good to be assured that they are the peers of everybody else. Honest effort should be praised and rewarded. It should not be mistaken for excellence. The distinction schools should make between leadership and followership ought not to take such form that leaders are represented as being better than others; but to talk about mediocrity as if it were superiority is to betray the chief end of private education. The energy and health of a democracy are based on differences in ability, not on the sophistry that because everybody's contribution may be equally worthy it is equally distinguished.

I have already dealt with the fact that elective positions in our schools are often awarded to students who, in the mature view, are not the best qualified candidates. The same criticism can be leveled against the occupants of the Presidency of the United States or against incumbents of high office in any field of human activity. It is not a valid argument against popular election to observe that it sometimes goes wrong. Only Fascists thoroughly believe so. And through the years, despite the propensity of Americans to become dazzled by prominence, undergraduate standards have been elevated, and over and over again popularly elected leaders have proved to be the best, to the confusion of my preliminary misgivings. The pursuit of leadership brings disappointment, sometimes painful, to the unsuccessful. "The spurns that patient merit of the unworthy takes" have need of fortitude. But it is not a bad thing to be beaten, and know why, and face it. Diversity of gifts is a fixed and conspicuous attribute of human nature. To learn to give what one can, responsibly and persistently, without bitterness or jealousy or regret; to recognize one's limitations and, in the light of them, to live devotedly and usefully—these are among the basic lessons of good citizenship.

The question of school discipline is a hotly debated one which deserves examination. In every phase of its social training the school has a central aim: to lead each student toward a sense of responsibility to the school community and an active promotion of its interests. Yet in pursuance of this aim the school is bound to encourage and give free rein to a wide range of individual capacities. The criteria by which it measures the presence or the lack of civic concern in its students must not represent a preconceived or stereotyped pattern. The terms in which it describes the desirable or the satisfactory must not exert a pressure toward conformity,

must not provide an incentive for conventional behavior. A
school must press for the full development of specialized and
private talent and then attempt to give it motive and direction
toward a social end. Its first duty is to the individual student.

But its duty to the whole school community is comple-
mentary and inseparable. A school's definition of standards
should be broad and flexible. But there must be general
standards; they must be clearly stated, widely circulated, and
thoroughly understood. Everyone must be bound by them.
The eccentricities of genius must not be exempt.

School discipline is synonymous with school morale. An
organization has sound morale if its members know exactly
what is expected of them, are determined to get it done, and
go about the doing with good heart and cheerful spirit. Such
an organization is well disciplined. The most effective incentives to good discipline, that is to say, are positive and
creative, not repressive or prohibitory. Good discipline is
constructive rather than negative. It is secured in schools by
giving students a combination of work and play which is so
presented as to seem to them worth their honest effort; by
holding them to high standards of performance; and by the
recognition and approval of work well done or well tried. It
is important that the standards be high enough to test the
capacities of the students. Nobody can be expected to do his
best at tasks which are made easy for him. The only consequence is boredom. Students may perennially protest that
their work is too difficult; but in a quarter century I have
known only two boys of real ability who transferred to
another school because it was easier, and said so. On the
other hand, I have known many who, having done their best
and failed, have expressed respect for the standards of their
school and their gratitude for the profit they had gained
from their experience.

With these familiar observations no one who has worked in schools will be likely to disagree. There is in every school, however, a group of students who lack either the ability or the inclination to meet the prescribed standards. The problem of inability accompanied by willingness and earnest effort is not hard to solve, though its solution causes disappointment and sometimes pain. Children who do their best and find it is not good enough deserve patience, sympathy, and admiration. No one should have the presumption or the heartlessness to suggest that they have failed. After hope and encouragement have had their day, such children are entitled to relief from their frustration through withdrawal and entrance into another school whose demands upon them they can adequately meet. Such a decision should be reached by conference among the school authorities, the parents, and the child. It should not be taken as a disciplinary or penal measure, but on the basis of clearly demonstrated reason and always with the single intention of the child's development toward a sense of confidence in his capacities. Except under special and compelling circumstances, such transfers should be made at the end of an academic year, so that the child can enter his new environment with others, at the regular time, and without the embarrassment or humiliation likely to be caused him if he changes schools during termtime. The peremptory dismissal of such students is a cardinal sin, for when a school accepts a pupil it accepts also an obligation to him, which it may not justifiably vacate until it has done all it can for him.

The temperature of educational controversy rises rapidly when it grapples with the problem of students whose capacities are adequate but who do not meet the requirements. Those of them whose difficulty is caused by emotional or personality problems are treated elsewhere in this book. They do not need punishment. They need a good doctor. They are vastly outnumbered, however, by those whose situation does not call for mental hygiene therapy, but does call, sometimes very loudly indeed, for whatever kind of treatment will provide them with an effective incentive toward responsible performance.

The school's obligation toward them is peremptory. It must exhaust the resources of persuasion, cajolery, admonishment. It must be ingenious and devoted and skillful in the interests of redemption. These failing, it must then resort to punishment.

The effectiveness of punishment depends on its being used rather as a last resort than as a preliminary threat, and on keeping its terms pretty vague. Some school rule books are so comprehensive and inclusive that they suggest an exhaustive and zestful appetite on the part of the faculty for multiplying the possibilities of misbehavior. Since no normal child could be expected to have thought of more than a few of them, they are likely to be regarded as an exciting introduction to the illimitable nuances of undergraduate depravity. Those with a taste for adventure are thereupon moved to the practice of what the military refer to as the "calculated risk," measuring pleasure against penalty with subtlety and finesse, straining at gnats when they should be laboring in the vineyard. The wisdom of experience suggests that the fewer the stated rules the better.

What is wanted is a firm statement of the sort of behavior and performance the school expects, the insistence that it be delivered, and the evident willingness to step in and take action when it is not.

The serious objection to a multiplicity of rules, of course, is not that it invites hairsplitting among adolescent lawyers. There are two important counts against it. One is that to direct the attention of students to a list of prohibitions, in-

stead of placing before them incentives to accomplishment,
is negative and suggests anxiety and suspicion on the part of
the faculty. The other is that discipline and morale cannot
be secured by rules, no matter how frequently and severely
they are enforced. This is a case of the inefficacy of external
force to control the minds and hearts of men. If the students
in any school took it into their heads to defy the authority of
its management, there is simply no coercive instrument by
which it could be maintained. And the very occurrence of
such a revolution would indicate that all that was worth gaining had been lost. In training young people for cooperative
citizenship, there is no substitute for the inculcation of an
inward sense of obligation and responsibility. A school's
standards can be upheld only through the voluntary agreement of its students that they ought to be upheld because
they are reasonable and necessary.

But boys and girls in school may be required to meet these
standards adequately if they expect to enjoy in full the
pleasures and privileges of the establishment. If the school
can be bound to provide the opportunities for social development, the students may properly be held to take advantage
of them—or lose standing in the community. A school is
under no obligation to keep a student who flagrantly neglects
his duty or whose behavior as a member of his group is
destructive of the ends that have been set before it. When
such a person offends, it is important to the good of the
institution that he be warned and, if it seems useful or necessary, restricted or punished, and that publicly, so that other
weaker brethren may be admonished. If all corrective measures fail, he should be dismissed, and it is frequently a salutary
thing to tell the whole community why. If the private school
is to be true to its mission—the encouragement of excellence
—then those who want its advantages but work against its

purposes cannot be tolerated. They are infectious, and they need to be excised. It is the experience of every teacher that, after such radical operations, morale rises and the school is a better place. For well-intentioned students have no real respect for an institution whose tolerance of the subversive is without limit.

Since dismissal is the last resort of all, and because its consequences are so severe for the victim and his parents, it ought to be preceded by the most patient and painstaking consideration. In this consideration, as in the case of all offenses against good discipline which may result in serious punishment, members of the student body should take part. The discussion should be confidential and unrestrained. The imposition of penalties by teachers alone can do serious injury to school morale. Young people and adults may have the same moral convictions and basic values. Yet their respective codes are colored by different weights and emphases, by a sense of different compulsions and responses, different areas of tolerance and understanding. An action of dismissal imposed by faculty decision may therefore seem to students unreasonable or unjustified, in view of feelings or attitudes or information which are theirs alone. In fairness to them, their views should be taken into counsel. Furthermore, undergraduate discussion of events leading to serious disciplinary action usually contains a degree of inaccuracy and unsubstantiated rumor. The presence of student representatives at all such discussions corrects error and keeps the story straight in the minds of the school body. Most important of all, a joint faculty-student agreement on the proper action to be taken on misconduct symbolizes the fact that the school's standards are the standards of the whole community and not merely of part of it.

All these principles and procedures in the social training

of young people are directed toward the establishment within the school of a certain moral climate, in which the citizens ought to feel freedom and stimulation rather than repression and fear. One of the purposes of avoiding a large number of fixed rules is to give them plenty of room to make mistakes. Too many teachers set undue store by *preventing* mistakes, thereby curtailing the opportunities for growth; for nobody ever profited by the mistakes he did not make. Though it is frequently remarked that experience is the best teacher, it is more important to observe that it is always a painful teacher. The value of error lies solely in its unpleasant and unforeseen consequences. Undergraduate mistakes, therefore, are the best texts schools can find for social education. And since discovered offenders against standards are usually chastened, they are ideally receptive to admonition and correction. If wise counselors then point out dispassionately the nature of the lapse, the reason why it is a lapse, and the desirability of avoiding it in the future, punishment is usually unnecessary and irrelevant. On one occasion I sent for an editor of the school paper who had inserted in a weekly column, for the purpose of filling the required space, an anecdote lifted from a college humorous magazine which was patently risqué. My attitude when he entered my office was one of righteous indignation. Almost at once I suffered the acute embarrassment of discovering that he had not got the point; and I felt like nothing so much as an aging roué as I found myself under the necessity of explaining it to him! I felt afterward that the guardianship of the standards of the community was perhaps not quite obviously in the right hands. Such experiences are an antidote to the brisk censoriousness to which all teachers are prey.

It follows that a proper social training program in a school should try to devise, in every aspect of a student's life, "social" situations in which the desired response will automatically be rewarded in a form which the student will understand and appreciate, and *within the context of his student life*; and the unsocial response automatically penalized within the same context.

Some critics of the private school assert that its training for citizenship is inadequate because it does not effectively inform and inflame its students about the pressing national and international problems of their day. It is unfortunately true that in these areas too many Americans are ignorant and unconcerned. The private school should certainly try to enlighten ignorance, and generally it does, through courses in history, civics, or what are unpalatably called "current events." In the teaching of American history the private school, furthermore, should not only present the facts but should attempt to inculcate an appreciation and an advocacy of the principles of American democracy, and an awareness of the threat to the security of these principles which other political and economic systems present.

But in so doing the school must never forget the fact, or fail to present and emphasize it, that truth and prejudice are antipathetic; and that its duty is to encourage the earnest and dispassionate pursuit of truth, rather than the arbitrary imposition of a specific body of beliefs. Furthermore, what sets group against group, race against race, nation against nation, is not systems but people. Many of us speak of "the government" as if it were a piece of machinery, imposed upon us externally, its deficiencies correctable by mechanical adjustments or changes in personnel; much as a man may turn a gadget on a balky furnace and then forget about it. The government is people. The enemy of peace, of the good life, is not machinery. It is fear, hunger, insecurity; greed, ignorance, hatred; intolerance and envy. It is these hateful qualities in men that schools should attack, from which they must set free their students. Much good can come from bringing into the consciousness of young people the problems of life beyond the limited, protected bounds of their school campus. It will not make them better citizens, however, if it diverts their attention and concern from the problems of their own school communities. For the destructive emotions at large in the world are present, all of them, on the grounds of every school. I have known boys who were admirably irate at the racial persecutions of nazism, who plainly exhibited racial intolerance in school; and Northerners who inveighed against white treatment of southern Negroes, but were contemptuous of New York Jews.

Every school has its own house to clean. It is a small house indeed, but it is also a community, with a common good to cleave to. Certainly the best assurance schools can offer that their graduates will be good citizens in their home communities is to make them alert, perceptive, intelligent, and conscientious citizens of their schools, which are their present life.

CHAPTER X

"Speak Roughly To Your Little Boy"

Private schools have been slow to recognize the relationship of mental hygiene therapy to the process of adolescent education. Psychiatry is still a comparative newcomer in the practice of medicine, and its popular reputation is, to say the least, uneven. To some laymen, doctors who set themselves up as being able to tell others why they behave the way they do are not scientists but charlatans. Some psychiatrists are charlatans (which does not remotely suggest that psychiatry itself is a hoax); but so are some physicians, surgeons, ministers, teachers, lawyers, and businessmen, whose occupations are generally looked at as being respectable pursuits. Others express no opinion about the scientific validity of psychiatry in theory, but make no bones about repudiating any body of thought which Sigmund Freud had a hand in shaping. These are the people who shudder at the fact that psychoanalysis often brings to the surface material which polite society regards as not very nice—a phenomenon with which Christianity has long been familiar. Then there are the confident extroverts who are so satisfied with the outcome of their own development that they scoff at the use of forms of therapy to which they themselves were never introduced.

These are likely to be the "normal" fellows, loath to accept the psychiatric dictum that nobody is normal and everybody a little bit neurotic.

The observation that one or two generations ago people got along all right without psychiatry (and why not now?) is scarcely instructive. It does not substantiate the view that they did not need it, but merely the obvious fact that they did not have it. A large number of people died of inflammation of the bowels before the diagnosis of appendicitis was perfected, and of diabetes before the development of insulin.

It does seem to be true, however, that the symptoms of emotional instability have been multiplied by the increasing tensions of life during the past thirty years or so. The emotional keynote of those decades has been uncertainty, which produces fear, nervous strain, insecurity. People have lost their money and their jobs—and, in war, their sons and daughters—and they face now a future of which nothing seems sure except that it will be hard and unpredictable. When it is remarked that all children born since the roaring twenties have known nothing else but such a tormented world, it is not surprising that their emotional equipment is frequently overtaxed.

Private schools above all, perhaps, might have been expected long since to trace adolescent behavior to its roots in personality. They are really just beginning to do it now. They have followed traditionally the Puritan conviction that all antisocial behavior is morally censurable and should be punished, and they have punished it without, until recently, giving serious attention to the reasons for it.

Perhaps the most familiar symptom of adolescent insecurity is stealing. The effect of stealing upon a school's morale is particularly disturbing because it breeds suspicion and distrust. If suspicion is directed against the innocent, the consequences can be not only painful but psychologically damaging. A quick discovery of the offender, therefore, is important for all concerned. Traditional procedure made use of marked and "planted" money, peepholes, decoys, watchers posted in closets or under beds, and other methods associated with a criminal investigation. If the culprit was caught red-handed, he was branded as a thief and returned to his parents a much worse problem than he was before. All teachers of twenty-five years' experience can remember such episodes and the way they were handled.

Today there is among teachers a growing awareness of the underlying emotional conflict of which stealing is the expression. More conspicuously than any other typical adolescent lapse, such as lying, stealing is a direct attack upon the school community. It is antisocial in the extreme. The moral guilt of a lie is conditioned by the circumstances surrounding its utterance. Theft is wrong in all situations, and everybody knows it. Everybody knows also, since theft is dramatic and spectacular, that its consequences are harsh, both in the punishment society imposes and in damage to the reputation of the thief. It is almost inconceivable, therefore, that a normally adjusted child would steal coolly and deliberately or as an act of pure bravado. In consideration of the risks involved, the adolescent thief, therefore, is offering convincing clinical evidence that he is in a state of emotional disturbance and needs therapeutic treatment. It is no good to tell him that stealing is wrong: he knew that before he stole. In fact, that is why he did steal. His stealing was a gesture of retaliation against a society in which he did not feel secure, which he felt had rejected him. It was a compulsive action which he could neither explain nor resist. Somehow it gave him the satisfaction of revenge, though he could probably give no satisfactory account of whom or what the revenge was directed against or why he felt he had to have it.

This diagnosis, if further confirmation were necessary, is substantiated by objective facts which seem to be common to episodes involving theft in schools. Though money is often stolen, I can remember no case in which it was money that the thief needed. Generally he had enough of his own. It is apparently not the intrinsic value of what is taken that gives satisfaction; it is the fact of possessing it, secretly and guiltily, that gives the compensatory thrill. I think of a boy who appropriated spare erasers for automatic pencils, of another who took magazines from the school mailbox, of a third whose specialty was paper clips.

Now, the Puritan tradition was not necessarily in error in its conviction that children who stole must be removed from their school communities. The serious repudiation of a school's basic standards often calls for loss of membership in the school body. But a school which dismisses a child for proven theft and does nothing else is merely getting rid of a problem, washing its hands of it, in a sense, rather than advancing its solution. It is passing judgment on a moral offense without realizing that it is also confronted by a form of illness. Those of us who are familiar with the resources of mental hygiene therapy would expect such an offender to keep on stealing until the reasons why he was doing it were made clear to him and, in consequence, the compulsion removed.

The experience of The Lawrenceville School with psychiatric advice began in the winter of 1947. Three boys who had been persistent and extravagant nonconformers had gone far to wreck the morale of their House. The Discipline Committee, including boys and masters, voted to dismiss them. After talking with the boys separately, I asked the Committee to withhold the imposition of the penalty in the case of one boy, recommend him to a psychiatrist, and consider the psychiatric report before taking final action.

When the Committee met again a few days later, all of us were curious about the psychiatrist's report, and most of us a little skeptical of its probable soundness, fearing that it would be overindulgent and sentimental in its attitude toward schoolboy misbehavior. His report received close attention; and when, at the end of it, the doctor recommended that the vote of dismissal be executed, the atmosphere thawed perceptibly! The session was long and interesting, marked by intelligent questions and fruitful discussion. For most of us, it was our first experience of a full account of the reasons for misconduct in a boy of attractive personality and superior ability. It gave us the why as an explanation of the what. It made us feel that maladjustment, recognized early enough and referred promptly to competent therapy, could be relieved before any question of possible dismissal had had time to rise.

A few months later a second boy, then in the eleventh grade, was referred to the psychiatrist because he was failing in all his academic work and his influence was felt to be demoralizing. The doctor saw him every day during the holidays and once every two weeks for the rest of the school year. In June he passed in all his subjects, and the next year graduated and went on to college. It was possible for him to understand remarkably quickly the causal factors behind his compulsions, and with their recognition came a release of tension and restored efficiency. There is no doubt in my mind that, without the therapy, he would have made a miserable failure of the year, and the necessity of his dismissal would have been obvious to everyone. At about the same time, the psychiatrist examined four more boys. Two of them, after the nature of their problems had been revealed, were advised to transfer to day schools in their home communities and continue treatment under local psychiatrists. The other two continued therapy but stayed in school.

On the basis of these encouraging experiments, when the new school year opened in the autumn of 1947, the psychiatrist was invited to deliver a series of lectures to the faculty. Attendance was made compulsory for the Discipline Committee and for Housemasters (some men were in both groups) and optional for the other masters. The lectures, in language aimed at laymen, described the crucial stages in the development of normal personality and then, drawing upon the case histories of Lawrenceville boys who had been treated (their names were withheld), made clear the kind of later emotional disturbance likely to exhibit itself if the main developmental adjustments had not been satisfactorily established. The faculty group also learned enough about the forms of behavior symptomatic of the most common types of emotional difficulty to permit them to recognize them when they saw them. The apparently well-adjusted boy who becomes a behavior problem and the boy of superior mental ability who collapses academically, in the absence of identifiable external causes, were cited as most likely to be candidates for mental hygiene therapy. The responsibility of the school to maintain high standards of discipline was given full emphasis. The limitations upon its indulgence of the individual which a school may observe without neglecting the interests of the whole group were recognized and considered. The new note was the psychiatrist's affirmation that serious and persistent misconduct is always a cry for help as well as an incitement to punishment.

We were cautioned against the dangers of coming to regard ourselves as part-time amateur psychiatrists, a role which I myself had repeatedly tried to play and had bungled conspicuously; and urged, when a situation rose which we thought needed attention, to seek professional assistance. It was repeatedly brought to our attention that mental hygiene therapy is not psychiatry, but preventive psychiatry; using the techniques of psychiatric analysis—but not of psycho-analysis—to nip potential disaster in the bud—a result made possible by the youth of the subjects and the consequence that their suppressed material lay close to the surface of their consciousness.

Interest in the lectures was keen and general. There were points of disagreement and skepticism, but these were brought out into the open and aired. There was an evident eagerness among the men to get more information on how they might helpfully attach themselves to the projected program. Some dissent to the whole concept there was, and still is; but an increasing number of masters, having seen the results secured, are cooperating with it. The reaction of the faculty is on the whole satisfactory in the opinion of the psychiatrist and of those masters closest to the process.

When mental hygiene therapy as a regular part of the school's medical regime was decided, its reception by boys recommended for it and by the student body as a whole gave rise to some apprehension. Some felt sure that a school psychiatrist would be generally referred to as the "nut doctor"; that boys would feel embarrassed at consulting him and jeered at for doing so; that to adolescents people who go to psychiatrists are somehow "crazy"; and that to do so them-selves was a confession that something was wrong with their brains. The apprehension was almost completely unjustified. At the beginning the school's weekly newspaper gibed once at the activities of the psychiatrist, but not a second time. Once a patient angrily declined further treatment after his first interview—a pretty clear indication that he needed help. From the outset, however, as boys who were treated became familiar with this hitherto unknown and rather upsetting process, and particularly as they discovered that they were getting help from it, they became increasingly aware of its importance to them in understanding themselves and others. It has never been difficult to persuade a boy of the advantage of consultation after its purpose has been made clear to him. Boys in emotional difficulties are puzzled and frustrated. They do not like to be the way they are. They want help. If they are persuaded that they can get it, they will take advantage of the opportunity. My observation is that the program is now accepted by the school, with perhaps an irreducible minimum of ignorant sneering.

An example of its acceptance by the undergraduates is provided by a boy who, on his own initiative, came to one of the administrative officers and asked for an appointment with the psychiatrist on his next visit to the school. Parental consent for the interview was obtained, and a time was set. The boy's parents were divorced and both of them had remarried. He had asked for help because of growing nervous tension and emotional instability: he cried easily without provocation, was depressed, and had a feeling of impending disaster. Therapy was discontinued because of the parental insistence that the patient was not ill enough to need it; though the boy's situation had been only partly relieved. But the fact that he had taken the first step without adult suggestion was encouraging.

The relationship of parents to a program of mental hygiene is of basic importance. No boy at Lawrenceville is referred to the psychiatrist until the consent of his parents has been received; not merely because the school feels obliged to get authority for the procedure, but because it is always desirable and sometimes essential that the parents participate in the remedial treatment. One of the most heartening features of the Lawrenceville program has been the eagerness of most parents to give full cooperation, frequently at the cost of valuable time and considerable inconvenience. It is hard to be told that one's son needs psychiatric treatment; it takes humility and fortitude to accept it, moral stamina and complete honesty to face the findings and establish within the family a new emotional relationship. For parents are more likely than boys to feel that psychiatric treatment carries with it a certain social stigma, a sort of skeleton-in-the-closet connotation. A greater difficulty stems from the fact that the seeds of a sense of insecurity or rejection, which may not come to the surface till adolescence, are always planted and take root during a child's earliest years; so that the emotional nature with which he emerges from infancy is the product of the subconscious emotional adjustments he has made with his parents; which is to say that it is the result of the way his parents have treated him. In consequence, the evocation of the causal factors that lie beneath conspicuous symptoms of insecurity and rejection is frequently painful. It is not surprising, therefore, that parents should find it difficult at times to face the facts; and it is greatly to their credit that so many of them are willing to do so.

Usually the parent-son relationship is mainly concerned with the child's adjustment to one of the parents rather than to both. The citation of a couple of specific situations, with alterations in factual details, will serve to enlighten the preceding generalizations.

A boy of fourteen was referred to the psychiatrist because of gross academic failure and continual misbehavior. His academic aptitude was exceptionally high. Obviously he was making no attempt to do what was required of him. In his classes he was inattentive and a distracting influence. He was constantly trying to show off; he talked incessantly, interrupted his teachers, was impertinent to them, was repeatedly dismissed from the room. He was untidy in dress and person, late for meals, and a chronic liar.

The boy was four when his father died. The few memories he had of him were pleasant. When the boy was six, which was eight years before the psychiatrist first saw him, his mother remarried. The boy declared that the new marriage was happily received by all concerned, and that therefore he had been happy about it too. In the course of the interview, however, he showed great resentment toward his stepfather, who he felt had taken his mother away from him. Both the mother and the stepfather talked with the psychiatrist. The stepfather, an intelligent, understanding man, tried to help as much as possible in the treatment of the boy and his problem. The mother, on the other hand, a nervous, tense individual, could not comprehend the meaning of her son's failure in behavior and academic work. When it was explained to her in dynamic terms, she accepted the interpretation only superficially, rejecting it in substance.

The boy himself was able to move toward the solution of his problem rather rapidly. He was of course perfectly aware of his misbehavior and of his failure to attend to his required school work, but he could not by himself alter the pattern. During treatment he was able to direct toward the doctor a great deal of the hostility he had felt toward his stepfather. As he did so he gained insight into the causes of his difficulty, his behavior improved, and be began to gain ground in his studies. During several subsequent interviews, the doctor continued his attempt to help the mother realize the meaning of the boy's behavior, and with some success. The boy made steady progress and passed all his work at the end of the year.

The following year treatment was not resumed because the boy's status in both studies and conduct was satisfactory.

Another boy of seventeen was referred to the psychiatrist because, again, of a combination of behavioral and academic deficiencies. He repeatedly called the attention to himself of boys and masters by breaking school rules. The boy came from a broken home. His parents were divorced; his father had remarried. The boy continued to live with his mother. He felt totally rejected by his father and stepmother. The father made only rare attempts to see his son, and these occasions were usually unhappy ones for the boy. His mother was absorbed in her own social and emotional satisfactions to the exclusion of a concern for the boy's welfare and interests.

During a series of interviews the boy indicated repeatedly that he felt his fellow students were aware of his home situation and that, although he was invited to many of their homes, he could never accept because he could not reciprocate the invitations. Because of his shame and anxiety about his family status, the doctor recommended that the boy be withdrawn from school and allowed to live at home, receiving further treatment from a psychiatrist in his home city.

The recital of such cases could go on indefinitely: two parents who were unaware of the part they had played in the production of a serious behavior problem; two boys whose families, with the best will in the world, had continuously thrown at them the superior accomplishments of a brother or sister, confirming them in a sense of inferiority; the boy who felt rejected by his father, who said of him, "My father's a fine man. I guess he just doesn't have time for me"; another instance of rejection in which serious misbehavior was limited to actions which the parent had specifically forbidden, flouting the school's authority as a symbol of the parent's.

One follows such adventures with a full measure of sympathy for the parents. A medical description of the causes of the symptoms of *physical* illness in a child may shock or frighten parents and engage their deepest emotions; but the facts of such a case are objective and neutral and outside of personality and conscience. The causes of mental and emotional disturbance, on the other hand, since they lie wholly within the personalities concerned, consist of actions and attitudes on the part of parents, well meant but misguided, unintentional and unconscious, but damaging to the child's security. It is bewildering to learn that love can issue in harm to the person loved, that the emotional and mental distortions of parents can become part of the fabric of their children's consciousness.

The realization that it can be so leads some parents to a sense of guilt, to the conviction that the child's difficulties are their fault. At other times parents resent what they take to be the implication that they are being blamed for a development of which they were entirely unaware. Both these attitudes are inappropriate. It is the intention of psychiatry, as it is of internal medicine and surgery, to discover causes and the effects that proceed from them and to apply the proper curative treatment. Psychiatry does not praise or blame on moral grounds. Professionally speaking, it brings the neutrality of scientific method to its techniques. Of course it offers sympathy to its patients, as all other branches of medicine do. Its only interest in feelings of guilt lies in getting rid of them by explaining what has produced them.

There is a feeling among some sincere Christians that psychiatry, in its probing of souls and its exorcising of guilt, is blasphemously usurping the province of redemptive religion. A person ought to feel guilty and sinful, they say, until he has surrendered his will to the will of God by the acceptance of Christ as Lord and Savior. It is impious, they say, to try to make a person self-reliant. He ought to rely on God.

But psychiatry does not deny these fundamentals of the Christian faith. It does not flout the truth of religion. By the use of methods of proved validity, it has developed a body of knowledge about the nervous, emotional, and mental life of human beings which is not available in any other field of thought; it can diagnose and describe and classify the types of mental illness; and very often it can cure it. It is true that a commitment to Christianity can at times resolve the fears and frustrations of a human spirit and give it unity and peace and force. But when it does, the conclusion to be drawn is not that the power of religion has refuted the value of psychiatry, but merely that the person benefited was evidently not in need of psychiatric therapy. A good many devout Christians lack emotional and mental stability, and it would be neither helpful nor correct to tell them that the reason was that they were sinful. Psychiatry does not deny religion's emphasis on the need for a conviction of sin. But when men and women become so obsessed with a sense of guilt that they cannot meet the demands of normal personal and social living, psychiatry has at its disposal resources to make the personality secure again. Security and self-reliance are relative terms. They cannot in any case be absolute. People in need of mental hygiene therapy are divided against themselves. When cause and effect are made clear to them, they are made at one with themselves, are given a sense of personal adequacy. The course of treatment, since it touches the mainsprings of human personality, is clearly concerned with the same dynamics as religion. But it calls them by different names. Psychiatry's province is science, not theology. The priest as confessor and the psychiatrist as analyst are both healers. In recognition of the similarity of their missions, theological students are commonly trained in psychiatry as well as in doctrine. The reforming of emotional relationships between parents and children calls for intelligent, unselfish cooperation. Self-reproach should have no part in it.

As the Lawrenceville program has developed, the psychiatrist spends approximately every third weekend at the school. He sees masters as well as boys. Frequently masters discuss with him boys who seem to them to be present or potential problems and are advised how to proceed without the psychiatrist's intervention. The parental role that housemasters play in the lives of their boys is an important one. For this reason it is felt to be advisable in some cases not to inject another figure into the situation. Through suggestions made by the psychiatrist to the masters, the boy is helped to gain sufficient insight into his immediate problem to ride out the storm. If the master fails to bring about an adequate change, the psychiatrist sees the boy. Some masters have sought advice about what their own attitude in the classroom ought to be in the handling of boys who they know are receiving mental hygiene therapy. Boys requiring more intensive treatment call at the psychiatrist's New York office once or twice weekly.

Teachers themselves, if they are good ones, regard their role as partly pastoral. They are keenly interested in the developmental progress of their students, including the moral and the spiritual, and they bring all their own inward resources to bear upon the problems of their students' lives. Frequently their pastoral concern, their sympathy and understanding, their wisdom, are all that is needed to give a student insight into his difficulties and strength to meet them. Some of them feel, therefore, that the cure of souls is wholly their responsibility, and that the use of psychiatry is a confession of the failure or the inadequacy of their own spiritual powers.

If the convenient accessibility of psychiatrists leads teachers to abdicate their pastoral obligations, the criticism is cogent. But that need not be so, and I have not found it to be so. And even if teachers exert the full measure of their capacities in the attempt to redeem a misguided student, there are two factors which limit their effectiveness from which they can by no means escape. In the first place, when behavior which may warrant serious penalties is in question, a teacher occupies not only a pastoral but a disciplinary role. He represents not only personal compassion but constituted authority. The error that excites his pity he must also judge. Knowing this, students may well hesitate to unburden their perplexities and bare their hearts before him. And in the second place, the layman who attempts to probe the depths of human motivation and impulse, to make his way through muddied waters, lacks the training either to ask the right questions or to rightly interpret the answers. By reason of these two limitations, as I know of my own experience, he may feel that he has resolved a conflict the nature of which he has not begun to discover; he may have aggravated the dilemma. As a curate of souls he had better prayerfully acknowledge his own limitations; and when he has gone as far as he confidently can, then, with no abatement of his sympathetic interest, he had better call for professional assistance.

What questions to ask and how to evaluate the answers are the stock in trade of the psychiatrist. As a repository of confidences, moreover, boys can go to him assured that he will be objective, uncensorious, with no interest in blame or reproach. Like a trusted teacher, his only purpose is to help; but he is free from the necessity of judging. In consequence, boys who, in repeated conversations with teachers have never gone beneath the surface of their troubles, have repeatedly, in response to skillful questioning by the psychiatrist, poured forth, during their second or third interview, historical, conflictual, anxiety-ridden material and have received, with only minor upset, his explanation of the cause and nature of their worries. There has never been any difficulty in bringing boys to realize that behavioral or academic failure was only the reflection of their conflicts, insecurity, or feelings of rejection. The abnormal has been quickly accepted as symptomatic of some underlying disturbance of a dynamic emotional nature. It has not been necessary in any instance to probe deeply for unconscious material. The work has proceeded on a fairly superficial level, describing to the boys the normal development of a personality and indicating the origins of their difficulties.

To the psychiatrist the most impressive feature of his experience has been the rapidity with which the therapy has progressed. Its intensive phase has rarely lasted for more than four to six weeks. After that period, which as a rule called for two or three sessions weekly, boys were seen once every three or four weeks on the occasions of the psychiatrist's visits to the school. When a boy had shown evidence that no further therapeutic help was needed, the interviews were stopped.

A striking factor of this psychiatric program has been the large proportion of the boys referred who came from homes broken by divorce or by the death of one parent or of both. They have accounted for 60 per cent of the patients. In cases where divorce has occurred, boys frequently have evidenced a feeling of guilt, of having been somehow responsible for the disaster. I think of this pathetic fact whenever visiting parents tell me they are divorced but that "fortunately it has done no damage to the children." Divorce always does damage to young children.

The use of mental hygiene therapy, some observers believe, contains the danger that it will become a crutch for the wayward; that all failure may be regarded as lying beyond the offender's power of control and therefore merits pity rather than censure. On one occasion at Lawrenceville, when the school had recommended therapy, the parental response was that there had never been any mental illness in their family and that what their son needed was not psychiatry but a sound spanking. If there is any danger of getting sentimental about failure, a school can only rely on the confidence it places in its psychiatrist. It is the school's responsibility to recognize that persistent failure by competent students may be caused by underlying emotional factors which need attention; it is the psychiatrist's responsibility to tell the school whether therapy is necessary or whether the usual methods of admonition and correction are sufficient. In the absence of mutual confidence, the relationship had better be dissolved. In the Lawrenceville experience the problem has not occurred. The psychiatrist has repeatedly acted as adviser, working through masters. And in cases requiring intensive therapy, he takes the view that the patient still bears a responsibility to the school's standards, which he may not continue to reject without the usual penalties. There has been a little evidence that well-adjusted boys who are meeting their obligations conscientiously are inclined to wonder why serious offenders are given what seems to them the unjustified dispensation of mental hygiene therapy. Sometimes a simple explanation of the situation suffices to dissolve the perplexity. That failing, the school had better risk occasional misunderstanding than withhold the kind of help it knows a boy needs. And it can reassure itself by the recollection of boys who have expressed gratitude for the help they have been given in finding their way from worry and despair and re-establishing themselves as happier, more stable, and more productive citizens.

CHAPTER XI

The Cornerstone

The Constitution secured once and for all the separation of church and state when it forbade the making of laws "respecting an establishment of religion." Instruction in religion is, in consequence, illegal in the public schools. Recently some public schools in some communities have "released time" for the instruction of children, on a voluntary basis, in the principles of their religions, under the auspices of their families or their churches. In Champaign, Illinois, such a program was sponsored by a Council of Religious Education made up of Protestants, Catholics, and Jews. An atheist, the wife of a professor at the University of Illinois, protested against the program, saying that her son was embarrassed at being the only student not participating. The Champaign School Board declared that a voluntary system involved no discrimination against atheists or in favor of any religion. Mrs. McCollum lost her case all the way through the Illinois state courts. She finally won in the Supreme Court of the United States, which decided by an 8-to-1 vote that the Champaign schools were violating the constitutional requirement of separation of church and state. The justices who favored the majority opinion were divided in their reasons.

There is an incidental irony in the fact that those who oppose most vehemently the reading of the Bible in the public schools are often unbelievers, who, having themselves rejected the validity of Christianity, would scarcely be expected to fear its effect upon their children. But the matter goes far beyond a point of irony. For the prohibition affects not merely instruction in religion; it has significance for education as a whole. It is perhaps hardly necessary for me to say that I favor the separation of church and state and that I should oppose, in our public schools, the attempt to secure belief in any religious creed or to attack any other belief, including the beliefs of agnostics and atheists. These are matters for which families and churches are responsible. But an education which excludes a knowledge of religion is a very different process, both in its methods and in its results, from an education which includes it.

Not many Americans are aware of the extraordinary diversity of practice in regard to the use of the Bible in the public schools; for not many of them stop to think that the constitutional prohibition of laws "respecting an establishment of religion" merely forbids a "state church" and has nothing to say about religion in education, which each state public school system has been free to treat as it pleased. In 1941 the United States Office of Education stated that in twelve states the law *required* the daily reading of the Bible in the schools, sometimes prescribing a fixed number of verses to be read without comment; in six states such reading was permitted; in eighteen others the law was so vague or its enforcement so inoperative that Bible reading was in effect permissible; in six states it was expressly forbidden; and in four more it was prohibited by inference. As the Committee on Religion and Education of the American Council on Education observes, the number of states requiring Bible reading is almost the same as the number forbidding it, though formal instruction is always banned. Sometimes religious instruction is conducted *in* the schools, but *by* and at the expense of church organizations. And many public schools stage Christmas plays or pageants. Meanwhile the general principle of "no religion in education" remains intact!

Being a nation heterogeneous in religious and national backgrounds, we undertake, in our educational program, no less a task than the making of Americans. We take pains to clarify what we call the "American tradition," and we try to inculcate "patriotism," not only through instruction but by the use of ritual and symbolism. We aim in this respect not only to inform the mind, but to stir the emotions and the imagination. Now, at the basis of the American tradition is the Hebrew-Christian tradition. The peculiar American emphasis on the special worth of every individual is not merely a democratic emphasis; it is a Christian emphasis. Yet, although we are permitted in our public schools to tell our children what it is, we are not permitted to study, as a matter of mere historical information, the document in which it is embodied. I have read the New Testament long enough, with groups of boys comprising Jews, Catholics, Protestants of various sects, and agnostics, to know that it can be done without theological debate or controversy and without attack, explicit or implied, on any special creed. Americans should know what Christianity is, and it is possible to teach what it is without offense. Furthermore, instruction in such fields as history and literature, which the public schools *are* free to offer, is so abundant in episodes and allusions which have a religious connotation that Biblical illiteracy is a serious barrier to their understanding and appreciation.

This is a matter on which there are wide and sometimes heated differences of opinion. A considerable number of intelligent and religious people regard the exclusion of Bible study from the public schools as being not only necessary but desirable. It is obviously necessary, but I do not regard it as desirable. I consider it a serious limitation on the value and effectiveness of public education.

To the extent that it is, the private schools are free from it. Certain of them, notably the Roman Catholic schools and some of the schools conducted by various of the Protestant communions, are definitely evangelical in purpose and procedure. They try to convert and confirm. The great majority of private schools are nonsectarian but avowedly Christian, though there is a wide diversity of view and practice as to the extent to which they are obligated—or well advised—to proselytize. Sectarian schools are generally attended predominantly by members of the particular faith they profess. They are in a special class; and since they generally know exactly what they want to do about religion, and are patronized presumably by those who want the same thing, I shall not discuss them here.

I do have something to say, however, about the position of the nonsectarian school that is avowedly Christian, for its position today seems to me to be equivocal.

It is hazardous and unprofitable to discuss in full detail the body of beliefs to which all Christians may properly be expected to subscribe or risk anathema. But it is possible to make an observation or two which most Christians would be likely to accept. One of them has to do with a major aim of formal education, which is the pursuit of truth. To the non-Christian, truth is present in the universe, and may be partially and increasingly apprehended by men who search for it. To those who discover it, it is useful in the degree that it seems to men to serve their purposes and to advance the "good life" as they define it. To the Christian, on the other hand, all truth is God's truth, which is related to man's good according to a plan and a purpose devised by God rather than by man. In consequence, to the Christian the fundamental ethical virtues, such as integrity and unselfishness and purity and love, are valid not because men have discovered, by practice and experiment, that they "work"; he believes they owe their validity to the nature and the destiny of man as God has ordained them. The Christian schoolteacher, if he is free to do so, will therefore regard Christianity as the frame of reference within which everything a man does derives its significance. He will not only hold to the conviction that instruction in religion is a necessary part of school work; he will take the view that all subjects of knowledge, even those which seem to be purely practical or utilitarian, are a part of God's truth and have a meaning in his plan.

There was a time—in my own experience it lasted till the impact and aftermath of World War I—when what I have said would have seemed a repetition of the obvious to private schools and colleges which were professedly Christian. Until then there was an institutional morality which was clear and unmistakable to the undergraduates. I am not saying that the old Adam was not active and effective on such campuses; my recollection is that he was extraordinarily hearty. I am simply contending that in that period, when you went to a private school or college, you knew what it stood for, religiously speaking; and the simple reason for that was that it did stand for something.

The political division of Western Europe following the Middle Ages, the rise of the merchant class, new concepts of the nature of man as a social, political, and economic being, broke up the medieval religious synthesis. A man's life became compartmentalized, secularized. The medieval concept that religious sanctions were operative in all aspects of living gave way to the notion that different sanctions were relevant to different aspects of living, of which religion was only one; that each field of human activity had its own inherent compunctions, which were not connected with religion. Secularism does not negate religion. It sidetracks it. It does not deny that religion is true. It denies that it is fundamental, or even relevant, to man's major concerns. Avowedly Christian education became secularized too.

In the college from which I was graduated just after the close of World War I, undergraduate protest against compulsory chapel was reaching its height, and soon afterward it was abandoned. I do not think it went by the board because undergraduate opinion had changed, though of course it had. I think it lost because the college as a corporate body no longer believed in what it still professed; and the undergraduates knew it. In other words, a point had been reached where institutional morality was no longer a body of corporate conviction; it had become simply the arithmetical total of the moral convictions of members of the faculty; which is to say that it had become nothing at all which had edge or bite or power.

The emergence then of the United States as the most powerful country in the world had something to do with the change; its material vigor and wealth, its industrial boom, Coolidge prosperity, two chickens in every pot, every man a king; if you were going to be rich beyond your dreams tomorrow, what did it matter what you believed today? Anyway, it happened; and today the problem is in the laps of Christian teachers everywhere.

The cause of Christian education today seems to me to be in worse case in colleges than in secondary schools. In all Christian communities, for example, common worship is a universal practice. I am fully and sympathetically aware of the difficulty, on grounds of freedom of conscience and opinion, of enforcing attendance at chapel upon a college undergraduate body which includes a wide diversity of race, color, and creed. Each Christian institution must decide for itself how the difficulty may best be met. I have a good deal of respect for those of them which have abandoned compulsion altogether, with voluntary religious services for those undergraduates who wish to attend them, and with an active program for the encouragement of Christian life and commitment on the campus. I see little merit, however, in the enforcement of attendance at chapel services part of the time, which seems to me to suggest that Christian worship is important enough so that everybody ought to be subjected to it now and then, whether it happens to mean anything to him or not; but that it is not important enough to make it a steady diet. This practice seems to me to be timid and inconclusive and unprofitable, as many compromises tend to be.

This is a problem which, as I have suggested, is less troublesome in private schools than it seems to be in the endowed colleges. In most private boarding schools, for example, there is compulsory chapel, both daily and Sunday. It is attended at Lawrenceville by representatives of the following non-Protestant faiths: Christian Science, Ethical Culture, Greek Catholic, Greek Orthodox, Hindu Brahman, Jewish, Jewish Reformed, Roman Catholic, and "no religious affiliation." The service itself is Protestant but nonsectarian. It seems to me to be instructive and encouraging as an example of unity of worship with diversity of faith—surely a consummation devoutly to be wished. Although undoubtedly some are present who, on religious or personal grounds, would prefer not to be, the number who have demurred explicitly during the past fifteen years has been negligible. The chapel requirement is known to every boy before he enters the school, and he is therefore free to accept it or go elsewhere. I suspect that the reason it works as well as it does is that it has always been basic in the school's purpose.

In Christian institutions of higher learning, and to a lesser extent in Christian schools, the question of religion is complicated by the principle of academic freedom. It is the stipulation of academic freedom that a college, for example, is in part a company of scholars banded together for the pursuit and the expounding of truth; and that whatever a scholar believes to be true he is at liberty to expound, without let or hindrance. Some advocates of academic freedom hold that if a scholar in pursuit of truth reaches the conclusion that Christianity is a snare and a delusion, his right to say so is inviolable and sacrosanct, though the institution that pays him may be committed to the Christian faith. Thus, in one reputable university, a professor announced to his students that the sacrament of the Lord's Supper was significant only as the example of a refined form of cannibalism; though he was not a professor of religion, and though his announcement, to the vulgar ear, suggests opinion, or perhaps prejudice, rather than truth. Controversy is good, diversity of opinion invaluable in education. Undergraduate ears should certainly not be protected from the intrusion of any ideas to which they do not already subscribe. Scholars must be permitted and encouraged to say what they believe and what they do not believe in their special fields. But professors sometimes use their academic chairs for *ex cathedra* utterances which would otherwise receive no attention, and they do so at times with unjustified finality. In their proper concern for scholarly objectivity, they seem at times loath to express a conviction. It is a problem of grave concern in the development of Christian education.

This question of academic freedom has a bearing, too, upon the religious responsibilities of nonsectarian Christian schools.

The catalogue of one such school, after stating that attendance at chapel and the study of religion are required, expresses the school's belief "that the divorce of moral training from its religious basis is sterile and destructive of the true ends of democratic living." In the words of former Chancellor Robert M. Hutchins of Chicago, as contained in a newspaper report, "Although it is theoretically possible to be moral without being religious, in practice it is impossible." The utilitarian view that man is the measure of all things, that the virtues underlying the "good life" are what man says they are, or what a consensus of "good" men agree upon, permits, if it does not necessitate, the adoption of a given moral code on grounds of expediency, however enlightened; and makes it difficult to denounce the morality of Hitler on any more substantial ground than that one does not happen to care for it. And though potential Fascists are relatively few in them, the private schools are entrusted with the nurture of large numbers of children who have pretty well absorbed the typical American gospel of "getting on in the world."

What are they to do about it?

A statement bearing on this matter was made a year or two ago in the *Alumni Quarterly* of Groton School by the Reverend Malcolm Strachan, a member of the Groton faculty:

Groton standards are, after all, not standards that were thought up in the seclusion of the studies of Groton masters; they are derived from scriptural admonition and teaching, colored and maimed necessarily by the personalities of the human interpreters here at Groton. Even a casual reading of the Gospels here at school would have forewarned a growing Grotonian that a life disciplined for high purposes is going to get pretty rough treatment at the hands of the multitude, and the Gospels would have forewarned him that a life of high principle is never a matter of adjustment with the world, but of constant conflict . . . One hears much talk of the business of adjusting oneself to the world as a kind of *summum bonum* of education; and that it is the duty of a school to arrange for the achievement of this. There is no scriptural support for such thinking . . . of coming to easy terms with the world, but always of getting into the midst of it to fight against and for it. . . .

The duty of a school is in reality to make its men more marked for the right reasons. The duty of all schools is to wipe away the fears of commitment to belief, the uneasiness of being "different"; and the yearning to be indistinguishable, to be undistinguished, to be one of the crowd, to be "adjusted," in the casual sense in which that phrase is ordinarily used, almost seem to be the deliberate aims of some modern educationalists in their desire to foster democracy. Anything which would appear to foster separateness instantly is labelled as "aristocratic" and not in tune with the times. But any man of belief and conviction is separate from his generation in any period of history, and "aristocracy" has nothing to do with that separation. We cannot have leaders without having men who are "different" . . . and where is the greatness of that school which does not help breed men who will risk the misunderstandings and brave the revilings and endure the conflict and loneliness for the sake of bettering His world in the name of Him whom to serve is perfect freedom?

The nonsectarian Christian school that accepts such a statement of its mission is bound to ask itself what qualifications and commitments may properly be expected of those who teach in it. If its students are drawn, as they very generally are, from various religious affiliations, a school is on sound ground with reference to its main function, which is to provide equality of opportunity to all whose qualities of mind and character commend them to it; and equality of opportunity means nothing important if it is limited to Christian believers. Those who teach in such schools ought also to include a diversity of religious background; and it is by no means necessary that it should be Christian, though Christian teachers and officials must determine policy and procedure in regard to religion. I am familiar with a faculty

which has occasionally furnished Roman Catholic leadership
for daily chapel and for participation in the teaching of religion, just as Protestant, Roman Catholic, and Jewish students
have conducted daily chapel. And I have known agnostic masters who, though their convictions made them feel that they
could not teach courses in religion, have been impelled to
volunteer their help to the religious program in other ways,
because they were convinced that the program was important.

Furthermore, I have known and worked with a considerable number of brilliant and fruitful teachers who have not
been convinced Christians; and I have not been able to observe that their influence academically was therefore weak-
ened, or to believe that it would have been enhanced by a
different set of religious convictions. Congeniality between
students and teachers on intellectual or aesthetic grounds is
often a rich and enlarging experience. A diversity of cultural
and religious backgrounds in students is responsive to an
equally various range of stimulus from teachers whose backgrounds differ too.

Teachers in a Christian nonsectarian school, however, may
properly be expected and required to assent to its main ethical
objectives and to support its religious program as fully as they
can. More damage is done to a school's religious objectives by
the failure of avowedly Christian teachers to attend its chapel
services faithfully than by the absence of a few agnostic
teachers who may be honestly seeking to deepen their perception of religious truth; for the failure of a faculty to support the religious program is promptly noticed by the students and is correctly interpreted as an expression of the
opinion that it is not important. Faculty negativism toward
the religious program is a problem in most nonsectarian
schools. Positive opposition to it cannot be tolerated. The
college professor who spoke sneeringly and contemptuously

of the Lord's Supper did violence to the religious convictions
of some members of his audience. If a schoolteacher made such
a statement, it should disqualify him, without any nonsense
about academic freedom. He has a perfect right to make
such statements as a person; but if he accepts a position at a
Christian school he has no right at all to make in the classroom religious affirmations which deny the validity of the
school's basic values, because he is bound to be listened to not
only as an individual but as a teacher with official standing
and sanction. This view does not constitute an abridgment of
freedom, academic or personal. It is an expression of the fact
that a teacher, when he accepts employment, undertakes
responsibilities as well as privileges; and to the extent that he
may derive prestige from his position he cannot properly use
it for the advancement of religious notions which the school
repudiates. Freedom of conscience and freedom of religion
and freedom of speech are fundamental rights, but they cannot be absolute and unqualified. I may pursue life, liberty,
and happiness as my right; but if I pursue them in such a
way as to infringe the equal rights of others, without scruple
or restraint, I will land in jail. And if I exercise my right of
free speech by conspiring to overthrow the government by
force, I have committed a crime. A concept of academic
freedom which is not limited by certain considerations of
morality and propriety is a dangerous and an insupportable
thing.

Because in this important matter I am eager both to be
understood and not to be misunderstood, I shall run the risk
of laboring a point by going further. Some readers may infer
from what I have said that I advocate forbidding teachers in
Christian schools to express any opinions about religion which
differ from those held by the "administration." I do not. On
the contrary, in regard to a school's program of religious

study, of chapel services, and of charitable activities, there should be a frank and full expression and discussion of the opinions of all the faculty, not at all as a mere gesture in the direction of the principle of free speech, but rather as the only way of formulating ends and means which will receive the support of the school community as a whole. Of course it would be impossible to coerce adults in such important matters even if it were desirable, which it is not. For coercion requires force, and force implies suspicion and distrust, and suspicion and distrust poison the atmosphere of the community. The emphasis should be placed on the establishment of a plan which the faculty will support because it is their own plan.

Beyond that, those teachers whose concern in the matter is deepest, and particularly the head of the school, should seek to deepen and enrich the influence of the plan in the school community. And if my own experience is typical, heads of schools could do more to bring reality to the religious life and to eliminate faculty negativism if they were more careful to examine the religious attitudes of candidates for teaching positions.

In a nonsectarian school the study of religion may not properly be dogmatic. The presence in the same classroom of Protestants of various sects, Roman Catholics, Jews, and members of other faiths or of no faiths makes it impossible, without grave offense to some, to insist that orthodox Christianity, and nothing else, is true. So much for the men and women who teach. If textbooks are used, care must be exercised to see that they do not express bias or prejudice; that they confine themselves to exposition, without attack. Because it is difficult to find books which are free of these faults, the best textbook is the Bible.

The primary end of classroom instruction in the Bible is

to find out what Christianity is by finding out what Jesus and the apostles say it is. And the record of the private schools in teaching this end falls far short of what it ought to be.

Two men who have been in charge of the religious life on the campuses of two important eastern universities commented recently on the results of religious training in the private schools. Speaking independently of each other and on different occasions, they had reached the same conclusion: in their work with college freshmen they had found a fair though uneven degree of Biblical literacy, and that was all. Graduates of private schools, they declared, exhibited an almost complete innocence of the knowledge that Christianity has an answer to the main problems that present themselves to undergraduates, and an equally definite conviction of man's obligations in all the relationships of his life. Much of their time and thought, they said, had to be devoted to the simple exposition of what Christianity has to say about the world today. Lacking this knowledge, undergraduates who had been brought up and wanted to continue to live as Christians were completely vulnerable to the winds of the materialistic, skeptical, or atheistic doctrines that blow across all campuses. Young men who "lost their faith" in college, they thought, did so not because it was inherently inadequate, but because they simply did not know what it was.

The evidence of these men is disheartening to those responsible for religious training in the schools, for it reveals the fact of failure at a crucial point. There is no reason to doubt the sincerity of those who plan their courses in the field of religion or to discount the careful thought devoted to making them as good as possible. Year after year, however, when religious education is discussed by private school teachers at national conferences, it becomes clear that no

other field of study generates as much perplexity and uncertainty among those who are concerned with its effectiveness. There is a fair degree of unanimity about the ends in
view, but a wide divergence of opinion about methods and,
fortunately, a healthy dissatisfaction and misgiving about
results.

Such discussions, weighed together with the testimony of
the two university chaplains, suggest some interesting speculations about the reasons for the inadequacy of the schools'
religious efforts.

It is hardly possible to believe that the subject matter of
courses in religion is primarily at fault. There is, to be sure,
a woeful paucity of books about Christianity which prove in
practice to be satisfactory at the secondary level; but the
situation would be little bettered if the need were filled.
Everybody who has taught such courses accepts the obvious
fact that the Bible itself is the basic document, and that parts
of it can be read and discussed with girls and boys in such
a way as to rouse interest and stimulate the re-examination of
personal religious beliefs. But to most teachers that result is
not enough to be satisfying.

A good deal of damage has been inflicted on the quality
and the acceptability of religious instruction in the private
schools by the fact that much of the teaching has been done
by men and women who were not sufficiently trained for
it—a condition which could have been corrected—and who
were neither interested in it nor committed to it—a far
graver fault, for teaching without conviction is worse than
useless. Wide participation by faculty members in the teaching of religion is desirable as a means of impressing on the
school body the fact that religion is a common concern and
not the province of an ordained clergy. But one reason why
most religious study does not engage the intellectual respect

or the honest effort of most secondary school students is
that it has been badly taught. What it needs is to become not
further clericalized but further professionalized; and to recruit for its practice those only who are genuinely interested
in it.

It is frequently pointed out by teachers that instruction in
religion may misfire because it begins at the wrong place. All
teaching, to be successful, must start where the pupil is, not
where the teacher wants him to be or thinks he ought to be.
Altogether too much pedagogical irritability is directed at
students by teachers who assume they understand, find out
that they don't, and lose their tempers over it. At the annual
meeting of the Secondary Education Board in Washington in
1950 Mr. Robert A. Moss of Groton School told the story
of a report on a book about penguins written by a boy in a
boarding school. "This," he confided, "teaches me more than
I want to know." We fail sometimes, Mr. Moss continued,
because we give answers to questions which are never asked.
And according to the university chaplains, we fail also to
provide answers to the questions students really do want to
ask, because we are so eager to tell them what we think they
ought to know.

In nonsectarian schools in which the study of the Bible
is required of all students, the objection is occasionally raised
that the version in use is not acceptable to some Christians,
or that the Bible, in any version, is in part or whole unac-
ceptable to non-Christians whose sacred writings are different. There is obvious logic in the objection, but it is largely
met as long as theological indoctrination or dogmatism is
avoided. Then the Bible, or parts of it, becomes a document of
historical and literary importance to children of non-Christian
faith, to whom it contains no religious significance. Most
children in American schools, moreover, intend to live in

this country; and since the Hebrew-Christian tradition has largely shaped its values, it is reasonable to concentrate on it even at the expense of other religious cultures and to ask non-Christians to study their sacred literature on their own initiative. For everybody alike, that is to say, the Bible is a part of our cultural heritage; and that education is deficient which ignores it.

The value of the study of the Bible as a cultural influence will of course be enhanced if its place in relation to other such influences can be traced historically under the direction of departments of social studies. The place of Christianity, for example, in the history of Western Europe, and the development of secularism and its causes, are matters of importance to educated Christians; and if no place can be found for such religio-social history in an already crowded curriculum, the recommendation of books to be read in supplement to Bible study would be better than nothing.

The program outlined above, which advocates, for the nonsectarian school, the study of the Bible on a non-doctrinal basis, and such additional historical study as may be practicable, will seem to some of my professional colleagues limited and inadequate; and I am inclined to sympathize with their misgivings, at least in part, for I should like to offer more. I have already recorded in this book my conviction that the purpose of all training is not merely to develop capacities (or, as in this case, to provide information) but to affect behavior. It will be urged against me here that the purpose of teaching what Christianity is is not to get people to know about it but to get them to do something about it. I should reply first that, in its academic presentation of religion, a *nonsectarian* school has to settle for what it can get, and that in the *classroom* all it can get is the nonindoctrinating approach.

But I should then maintain that *from* that approach the students will be bound to get much more than information. The only very widely used book I know of from which information only can be derived is a telephone directory. No one can read a great novel or play or poem without feeling an enhancement of his perceptions and insights, his emotions and imagination, his understanding and compassion. Great literature has a shaping, often a transforming influence upon its readers. Commune with Shakespeare, Keats, Hardy, and you are never the same person again. And you are not merely different; you are bigger, more of a human being.

Well, the Bible is very great literature indeed, and it has had the effect upon its readers, devout or otherwise, that great literature always has. I cannot conceive of anybody's studying it without feeling the overpowering stature of its thought and language, or without yielding in some measure to the mastery and might of the prophets, the apostles, and the Lord Jesus Christ. I have never known anyone who, in consequence of his study of the Bible, lost his interest in Christianity, though many have gained it that way.

The place where nonsectarian Christian schools may preach the fundamentals of Christian faith is in the pulpit. Ordained ministers and laymen, including members of faculties, may usefully be employed to this end. The basis of selection of school preachers should be Christian conviction and earnestness, and the ability to present them effectively in public: qualifications scarcely more often found in the clergy than in the laity. Something unfortunate happens to some ministers and laymen when they get up to preach to schoolboys. Some of them go overboard in trying to make the boys laugh; and though I concede that Christianity should be gay and joyous, I do not think it is funny. Others seem almost to identify positive convictions with bad manners or revivalism and in consequence present religion as if it were an interesting subject for inconclusive after-dinner conversation among gentlemen. If other heads of schools have erred as I have, they have not paid sufficient care to the selection of men really qualified to occupy their preaching function.

Through its chapel services, the private school is free, as the public school is forbidden, to preach the Christian religion. This preaching has both an educational and a religious value. It is educational to the degree to which it informs young people of what Christianity is, and thereby supplements the objective classroom study of the Bible; and it is educational also, in a period characterized by books and articles and speeches undertaking to bring spiritual comfort without pain or effort, as it makes clear to students what Christianity is not. In the fulfillment of its religious function, school preaching can help to overcome the limitations of impartial classroom study of the Bible by presenting the dynamic force of religion and by trying to lead its hearers toward an active, personal response to it. It can teach what faith is and urge its hearers to develop it. It can try to move them as well as to inform them. It can appeal to them to give themselves to a cause greater than themselves. It can urge them beyond knowing about religion to doing something about it. It can provide power to enliven facts. It can raise basic questions about the meaning of human life, and it can suggest answers.

In a Christian nonsectarian school, preaching may do these things with propriety and fervor. In doing so, however, it must never forget that its audience *is* composed of representatives of several sects and faiths, and it must avoid prejudice and contemptuousness with great care. I have known preachers, forgetting the need for this compunction, to give justified offense to Roman Catholics, Jews, and certain Protestants by flippant or illiberal or biased statements. But the line that must be taken is not hard to follow, and it does not require preachers either to dilute or to suppress their religious convictions. It requires courtesy and consideration and good will, which are Christian virtues.

There is one last opportunity open to the private school which completes its religious responsibilities.

In a good many such schools—chiefly the boarding schools, I suspect—there are so-called "school churches." They are not "churches" at all in the usual sense, for they belong to no formal sectarian organization and have no official standing. They are membership bodies, composed of those members of the student body who wish to ally themselves with others, including adult members of the school community, in a Christian fellowship. For some students membership in the school church is the first step toward a full church membership later. Others who are already church members join it as a church "home away from home," membership terminating on graduation. It can sponsor voluntary religious services at various seasons in the church year, general communion services at intervals during the school year, campus community chest campaigns, old clothes collections, and so on. The campus influence of such a school church is limited by its very nature. But it is useful as a symbol of Christian fellowship and as a reminder of the responsibilities and the opportunities of Christian life.

Religion, therefore, is the rock on which the whole program of our schools should be set, and freedom to make it so is the unique privilege of the private school; not a dogmatic or sectarian or creedal insistence; but the recognition that there is a power outside and above man of which he is the creature, not the creator, the servant rather than the master. The educated person is one whose innate capacities have been

trained, sharpened, enhanced, *and directed;* who feels an
obligation to devote himself to ends and purposes beyond
and above self-interest. Secular education deceives itself
if it believes that teaching, whatever the subject matter, can
proceed from no point of view. All teaching is conversion.
Education implies and intends conversion. The private school's
entire offering, not merely the forms and instruments of its
religious training, is its answer to the root question that it
must perennially ask itself: To what shall our students be
converted? If it asks the question with humility and executes
the answer it receives with energy and intelligence and faith,
the American democracy will heed it and uphold it and thank
God for it.